The Complete Wedding Planner

Avon Books are available at special quantity discounts for bulk purchases for sales promotions, premiums, fund raising or educational use. Special books, or book excerpts, can also be created to fit specific needs.

For details write or telephone the office of the Director of Special Markets, Avon Books, Inc., Dept. FP, 1350 Avenue of the Americas, New York, New York 10019, 1-800-238-0658.

The Complete Wedding Planner

A Month-By-Month Countdown To A Perfect Wedding

Suzanne Kresse

AVON BOOKS ◆ NEW YORK

* DEDICATION *

To my wonderful children,
Mike-Paul-Lynn-Laura,
who have always believed in me

THE COMPLETE WEDDING PLANNER is an original publication of Avon Books. This work has never before appeared in book form.

AVON BOOKS, INC.
1350 Avenue of the Americas
New York, New York 10019

Copyright © 1991 by Suzanne Kresse
Cover photograph by Jeffrey Edwards
Interior Design by Michaelis/Carpelis Design Assoc. Inc.
Wedding Gowns courtesy of Bridal Originals Inc.
Tuxedo photographs courtesy of After Six Formal Wear
"Marriage Laws" chart courtesy of The World Almanac & Book of Facts, 1991 edition, copyright © 1990 by Pharos Books, New York, New York 10166.
Published by arrangement with the author
ISBN: 0-380-76374-5
www.avonbooks.com

Library of Congress Cataloging in Publication data:

Kresse, Suzanne.
    The complete wedding planner : a month-by-month countdown to a perfect wedding / by Suzanne Kresse.
    p.   cm.
    1. Wedding etiquette,   2. Weddings.   I. Title
BJ2051.K73   1991   91-23270
395'.22—dc20   CIP

First Avon Books Trade Paperback Printing: November 1991

AVON TRADEMARK REG. U.S. PAT. OFF. AND IN OTHER COUNTRIES, MARCA REGISTRADA, HECHO EN U.S.A.

Printed in the U.S.A.

QPM 20 19 18 17 16 15 14 13

Table of Contents

Introduction

You are the bride of the '90s. You're smart. You're conscientious. You're seeking quality—therefore you shop and compare. You want only the best for your wedding. THE COMPLETE WEDDING PLANNER is *the* planner of the '90s. It's functional. It's comprehensive. It's complete. I have designed it for the busy bride like you, who needs to be organized.

Most important, it's *different*.

For ten years I have earned a national reputation for giving brides "advice that works." In 1981, I founded *Bridal Guide* magazine, a publication that I developed as the "How-to for I DO." Since that time, I have been appearing at bridal fairs across America, meeting and speaking to thousands of brides who all want the same thing—a perfect wedding!

This book you hold in your hands is my answer to your number one question, "How do I plan the most important day of my life?" The Planner is divided into twelve chapters representing the twelve average months of wedding preparation. Each chapter features a monthly countdown calendar that will organize your planning activities. This unique format can be used every day to keep your notes, appointments, and special details in order. It's everything you have been looking for to plan a traditional wedding—with a fresh approach.

Best Wishes,

Suzanne Kresse

Suzanne Kresse

Month of: _____

SUNDAY	MONDAY	TUESDAY	WEDNESDAY	THURSDAY	FRIDAY	SATURDAY
____	____	____	____	____	____	____
____	____	____	____	____	____	____
____	____	____	____	____	____	____
____	____	____	____	____	____	____
____	____	____	____	____	____	____

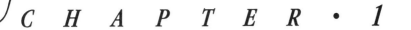

C · H · A · P · T · E · R · 1 ·

MONTHS BEFORE

Engagement Guidelines

From the moment you say "yes," your engagement officially begins. Check off each detail as you complete this part of your wedding planning.

☐ First, announce your marriage plans to both sets of parents or guardians.

☐ If parents live away, plan a visit in the near future.

☐ The groom's parents should call the bride's parents to arrange to meet and begin the initial planning.

☐ Next, inform any children concerned.

☐ Tell supervisors and co-workers.

☐ Tell family and friends.

☐ Set the date.

☐ Send an announcement to the newspapers.
Announcement should be printed near or on the date of the engagement party if possible. The announcement can appear three months to one year before the wedding.

☐ The bride's parents usually host an informal engagement party.

☐ Party guests should be limited to immediate family and close friends.

☐ Invitations can be written or verbal. Pre-packaged invitations can be used.

☐ At the party, the engagement is officially announced as part of a toast given by the father of the bride.

☐ The groom usually responds with another toast.

☐ A written thank-you or a small gift should be sent to the party hosts.

☐ Thank-you notes should be sent for any gifts received.

Engagement Announcement Form

To appear _____   Bride's mother's name_____
                    date   Telephone Number (daytime)_____
                               RELEASE DATE_____

Name of bride in full_____

Home Address_____

Telephone Number_____

Name(s) and residence(s) of bride's parents

_____

_____

_____

Name(s) and residence(s) of groom's parents

_____

_____

_____

Bride's schooling and present position

_____

_____

Groom's schooling

_____

_____

Groom's military record and/or present position

_____

_____

Expected Wedding Date_____

Make a copy of this page, and fill in all of the information. Be sure to check spelling. If you wish to include a photograph, send either a 5x7″ or an 8x10″ black and white glossy photo. Be sure to write your name, address, and telephone number on the back of the photo. Send all information to the society editor of your newspaper. If the groom's parents live in another city, send a duplicate copy of this information to them or directly to their newspaper.

$\mathcal{T}$ips on Ring Buying

- Shop only at reputable and knowledgeable jewelry merchants.

- Shop around and compare.

- REMEMBER—three weeks' salary or six percent of your annual income is the amount you should be budgeting for the ring.

- Tell the jeweler your price range.

- Get a written guarantee of the stone's value.

- If you finance the purchase, check several lending sources for the most favorable borrowing terms.

- Get a separate written appraisal.

- If your appraisal does not agree with the price you paid, return the jewelry for a full refund—fast!

$\mathcal{K}$inds of Weddings

Formal

- Engraved invitations

- Fifty to five hundred guests

- Afternoon or evening ceremony held in church, synagogue, or hotel

- Lavish reception with full meal and beverages served

- Music and dancing provided

- Six to twelve bridesmaids

- Bridal attire is elegant floor length with long sleeves, full train, and veil

- Groom wears: Afternoon—gray stroller coat with striped trousers Evening—black cutaway coat with tails

- Extravagant floral bouquets and decorations

Wedding Gowns courtesy of Bridal Originals Inc.

Semi-Formal

- Printed invitations

- 100 guests

- Ceremony held any time of day in church or private home

- Reception with food and beverages appropriate to the hour

- Two to five bridesmaids

- Music and dancing optional

- Bridal attire is fancy floor length with sweep train and veil or hat

- Groom wears formal tuxedo

- Floral bouquets and full decorations

Wedding Gowns courtesy of Bridal Originals Inc.

Informal

- Daytime ceremony held in church, private home, or judge's chambers

- Reception with hors d'oeuvres and beverages

- Maid or matron of honor and best man are only attendants

- Music optional

- Bridal attire can be tea length gown or suit with hair ornament

- Groom wears dinner jacket and trousers or fancy dress suit

- Simple flowers

Wedding Gowns courtesy of Bridal Originals Inc.

New Ways to Wed

Wedding celebrations that include unique themes can add a whole new dimension to your wedding day. Consider these ideas.

AN ETHNIC WEDDING
Includes traditional costumes, music, dances, and food. (See chapter 9).

A WINTER HOLIDAY WEDDING
Includes seasonal accents and decorations, velvet dresses, fur trims, and carol singing.

A MILITARY WEDDING
Includes the traditional arch of swords; groom and attendants wear full military uniform.

A WEDDING IN A MANSION
Includes turn-of-the-century gowns and morning coats. Butlers serve food and drinks. Violin music is played. Bride descends staircase. Wedding dress is antique ball gown with hoop skirt.

A GREENHOUSE WEDDING
A gazebo is used. Flower print bridesmaids dresses; real flower wreaths in hair. Many floral decorations.

A SPORTS THEME WEDDING
The couple marries on the court floor or in a gym. Sports decorations are used. Wedding party wears tennis shoes.

A ROYAL SEND OFF
A cannon is shot off as the bridal couple exits to their limousine.

AN ART DECO WEDDING
1920s costumes and decorations are used. The color scheme is black and white.

A SHIPBOARD WEDDING
Hire a cruise ship, and use nautical decorations. Provide live music as the ship cruises along harbor.

"PERIOD" THEME WEDDINGS
Costumes and trivia from 1920s through 1960s are integrated into the wedding ceremony and reception.

A PARK WEDDING
Includes picnic tables, grilled food, games, and casual attire.

AN ORIENT EXPRESS WEDDING
Marry on a train. Meal is served by porters on candlelit tables. Formal attire is requested, and music is provided by a harpist or strolling guitarist.

A WESTERN WEDDING
Western costumes are worn, country western music is played, barbecue meal is served on tables with checkered tablecloths.

HISTORIC PERIOD WEDDINGS
Entire wedding features a past era—Renaissance, Medieval, or Victorian—complete with costumes and decor.

THE WEEKEND WEDDING
Wedding celebration includes a festival held over several days. Activities begin with the rehearsal dinner held the day before the wedding, and they end with a brunch on the day after the event.

THE SURPRISE WEDDING
Invite guests to a party. Only when they arrive do they realize that they are actually attending your wedding. A unique second marriage idea.

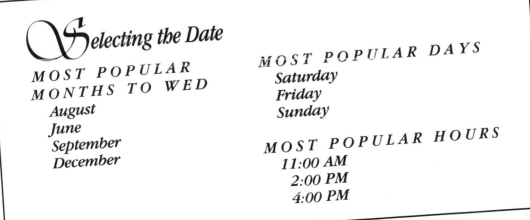

Selecting the Date

MOST POPULAR MONTHS TO WED
- August
- June
- September
- December

MOST POPULAR DAYS
- Saturday
- Friday
- Sunday

MOST POPULAR HOURS
- 11:00 AM
- 2:00 PM
- 4:00 PM

Wedding Costs

Never before have weddings been so lavish, lovely, or so expensive. The wedding of the '90s is an occasion for which costs are budgeted. These costs are shared by the two families that are being joined together. Any agreed upon responsibility for payment between family members is acceptable. The traditional division of wedding costs is as follows:

The bride and bride's family pays for:

Invitations and Announcements
Bride's wedding dress, veil, and accessories
Engagement and wedding photographs
Ceremony fees including site rental, organist, and soloist
Limousine or transportation for entire bridal party
Rental of supplies and equipment
Complete reception costs including food, beverages, music, and decorations and
    all gratuities
Groom's wedding ring
Groom's wedding gift
Gifts for all women attendants
Accommodations for out-of-town bridesmaids
Bride's personal trousseau and stationery

The groom and groom's family pays for:

Bride's engagement and wedding rings
Marriage license
Clergy members' fees
All wedding flowers
Bride's wedding gift
Gifts for ushers and groomsmen
Accommodations for out-of-town ushers and groomsmen
Complete honeymoon trip
Rehearsal dinner
Refreshments for reception (optional)

Attendants pay for:

Their entire attire for the wedding
Any travel costs
A wedding gift

WEDDING EXPENSE	TO BE PAID FOR BY:	ESTIMATED COST
Bridal Attire		
Invitations/Wedding Stationery		
Bride's Trousseau		
Bride's Rings		
Engagement Party		
Clergyman's Fees		
Groom's Attire		
Ceremony Fees/Organist/Soloist		
Groom's Rings		
Limousine		
Bridesmaids' Luncheon		
Bachelor Party		
Rehearsal Dinner		
Reception Site Fee		
Reception Catering		
Reception Refreshments		
Wedding Cake		
Music/Entertainment		
Photographer		
Video		
Florist		
Attendants' Gifts		
Honeymoon		
Wedding Gown Cleaning		
Attendants' Accommodations		
Rental Equipment		
Marriage License		
Decorations		

# *Our Wedding Costs*

Here is a *new* way to calculate your wedding costs *before* you begin. The chart below lists all of the details of the average wedding. It also lists what percentage that detail should cost. Fill in the estimated total cost of your wedding at the top. Figure each percentage of that estimate. *Use those as your buying guidelines.*

The national averages listed are based on a national average total cost of $15,000.

OUR ESTIMATED TOTAL WEDDING COST IS $_____

WEDDING DETAILS	THE NATIONAL AVERAGE	%	OUR WEDDING COSTS	RECOMMENDED BUSINESS TO USE:
Bridal Attire	$ 750	5%		
Wedding Rings	$ 2,250	15%		
Invitations	$ 600	4%		
Ceremony Fees	$ 150	1%		
Reception Costs	$ 5,250	35%		
Photography/Video	$ 1,500	10%		
Pre-Wedding Parties	$ 450	3%		
Groom's Attire	$ 150	1%		
Limousine	$ 300	2%		
Wedding Cake	$ 450	3%		
Attendants' Gifts	$ 300	2%		
Rehearsal Dinner	$ 300	2%		
Flowers	$ 1,500	10%		
Music/Entertainment	$ 600	4%		
Decorations	$ 450	3%		
TOTAL	$15,000	100%		

Keep track of all your receipts and contracts by placing them in a large specially marked envelope. Label each envelope according to the categories below. Separate and file all receipts in each appropriate envelope.

CATEGORIES

1. Ceremony and Invitations

2. Wedding Party and Attire

3. Reception and Wedding Cake

4. Photographer, Video, and Newspapers

5. Flowers, Music, and Entertainment

6. Honeymoon

$\mathcal{O}$ur Wedding Outline

Kind of Wedding: (circle one)   FORMAL   SEMI-FORMAL   INFORMAL

DATES: Day of Week   Date   Year

               1ST _____   _____   _____

               2ND _____   _____   _____

               3RD _____   _____   _____

Ceremony Time: Morning   Afternoon   Evening   (circle one)

1ST_____ 2ND_____ 3RD_____

Number of guests to attend (estimate): _____

Number of women attendants: _____

Names: _____

Number of men attendants: _____

Names: _____

Bridal gown description: _____

_____

Groomswear description: _____

_____

Color scheme: _____

Ceremony site(s) we like: _____

Reception site we like: _____

Meal will be: Sit-down Dinner_____ Buffet_____

             Cocktails and Hors d'oeuvres_____ Punch and Cookies_____

             Other_____

Reception Time: From_____ To_____

Music_____ Dancing_____ Alcoholic Beverages_____

Special customs and traditions I want included:

_____

_____

_____

What is the total amount we want to spend?__\$_____

Special Notes About This Month's Details

Month of: _____

SUNDAY	MONDAY	TUESDAY	WEDNESDAY	THURSDAY	FRIDAY	SATURDAY
_____	_____	_____	_____	_____	_____	_____
_____	_____	_____	_____	_____	_____	_____
_____	_____	_____	_____	_____	_____	_____
_____	_____	_____	_____	_____	_____	_____
_____	_____	_____	_____	_____	_____	_____

MONTHS BEFORE

The Wedding Party

•

The Guest List

•

The Ceremony Site

•

Reception Arrangements

•

The Photographer

•

Wedding Videos

The Wedding Party

Guidelines for selecting your attendants

The "wedding party" is really appropriately named. It is those people you invite to be your attendants who will make your wedding the best party of your lives. These special people should be asked in a personal way, allowing plenty of time for them to make all necessary arrangements.

Remember, it is a special favor to you that they are accepting this responsibility, added expense, and the time that their participation will involve.

THE HONOR ATTENDANTS

These special attendants may be married or single, young or old, male or female. A mother or father may also serve as an honor attendant. They must be twenty-one years of age, because they serve as the two witnesses required by law to sign the marriage certificate.

The Maid or Matron of Honor

This role is filled by the bride's sister or closest friend. She assists the bride with all pre-wedding details. During the ceremony, she arranges the bride's gown and train after any movement. She also provides the bride with the traditional "something borrowed" and "something blue."

The Best Man

This role is filled by the groom's most trustworthy friend or relative. His brother, cousin, best friend, or father are all appropriate choices. The best man assists the groom with all pre-wedding details. He escorts the groom to the church and holds the marriage license and ring during the ceremony. He delivers the officiant's fee and proposes the first toast at the reception. His last official duty is to arrange the newlyweds' departure for their honeymoon.

BRIDESMAIDS

The bridesmaids are chosen from among friends and relatives. This includes sisters, cousins, and sisters of the groom. Pregnancy no longer disqualifies a bridesmaid, as long as the bride and the mother-to-be are comfortable about it. Bridesmaids are required to attend all pre-wedding festivities. On the wedding day, they usually dress together, or they meet at the bride's home and then accompany her to the church.

USHERS

The groom may choose his brothers, cousins, or close friends to serve as his ushers. He may also ask the bride's brothers or cousins.

The main responsibilities of the ushers are:

• Seat guests at the wedding ceremony.

• Escort members of the wedding party.

• Direct guests throughout the reception.

• Two ushers also arrange a white cloth runner down the center aisle prior to the beginning of the wedding processional.

• The head usher escorts the mother of the bride to her pew. This officially begins the wedding processional.

CHILD ATTENDANTS

A *junior bridesmaid* is usually a sister of the bride or groom, ages eight through sixteen years. Her duties and privileges are the same as other bridesmaids. In the wedding processional, she precedes all other bridesmaids.

The *ring bearer,* who may be a boy or a girl, carries a white lace-trimmed pillow on which a fake ring has been sewn. The ring bearer can walk alone immediately preceding the flower girl, or the two may be paired and walk immediately preceding the bride.

Pages (bridal train bearers) always walk in pairs and are about the same height. They are usually dressed uniformly and can be either boys or girls.

Candle lighters, usually boys, step forward to light candles before the mother of the bride is escorted to her seat.

The Guest List

Guidelines for organizing your list

♦ Start compiling the list as soon as the engagement is announced.

♦ Every wedding guest list is divided into three parts:
  Bride's family and parents' close friends
  Groom's family and parents' close friends
  Friends and business associates of the wedding couple

The Card File Method

This method provides a quick way to locate a name, tabulate the guest count, and avoid any duplications.

MATERIALS NEEDED: Plain white 3x5″ cards
  One set of alphabetical index cards
  One file box

♦ On each card, write each name as follows:

  Last name, title, complete given name: Adams, Mr. and Mrs. John

  Complete address
    (as it appears on the invitation):   756 West Clover Parkway
                                         White Plains, NEW YORK 10034

  Names of children (under 18) at home: Martha
                                          Elizabeth

                                          769-3044
  Telephone Number:

♦ The cards are then filed alphabetically in the file box.

♦ As the responses arrive, mark the top right-hand corner of each file card with either an "R" for regrets or an "A" for acceptance followed by the total number of people who will be coming in parentheses—A(4).

- Each name on the list should be complete with full address and telephone number. This is important if you need to contact any late respondents.

- Set a deadline for the completion of the list.

- Regarding children—only the brothers and sisters of the bride and groom must be invited.

- Anyone invited to the ceremony should be invited to the reception. But, you may invite more people to the reception than to the ceremony.

- Invitations should be sent to all members of the wedding party and their parents.

- The officiant and his wife should be sent an invitation.

- Draw up a tentative list on the following page.

If you have too many names on your list, eliminate in the following order:

1. Business associates
2. Parents of the attendants
3. Second cousins
4. People who live more than two hours away

IMPORTANT PEOPLE TO INVITE

Name:	Address:	Phone:

The Ceremony Site

Site _____

Address _____

City/State _____

Telephone _____ State _____ Zip _____

Name of Officiant _____

Selected Date of Ceremony _____

Selected Time of Ceremony _____

Regulations concerning the day or time of day to hold the wedding

_____

_____

Church requirements for marriage _____

Special requirements for divorce or mixed marriage _____

Rehearsal Date _____ Rehearsal Time _____

Number of guests site can accommodate _____

Do special vows need to have approval _____

Restrictions on music _____ _____

Restrictions on decorations _____

Flowers _____

Accessories provided and fees for use of:

   Candelabra $ _____ Candles $ _____ Candle lighters $ _____

   Arch $ _____ Kneeling bench $ _____ Flower stands $ _____

   Guest book stand $ _____

Rules regarding photography _____

_____

Designated room for photographer to take pictures _____

Is there a sound system for recording the wedding _____ Fee $ _____

Facilities for the bridal party _____ Restrooms _____

Designated room for the bride _____

What is the fee for the use of the building $ _____

For the officiant $ _____

What are the additional charges for using the site for a reception $ _____

23

Reception Arrangements

RECEPTION SITE

The following two sheets will allow you to get several estimates for the reception site. Call and arrange appointments with the banquet managers. Take time to compare costs, facilities, and services. Confirm all details including costs, date, time, extra services, and menu in *writing*.

Any reputable establishment will happily provide an itemized contract for you. Be prepared to pay a ten to fifteen percent deposit when you sign the contract. Also inquire when the balance of the bill is due. Be sure to set a deadline for notifying the caterer with the exact number of guests who will attend. Usually this date is within one week of the wedding.

ESTIMATE SHEET

SITE DETAILS	SITE #1	SITE #2
Name		
Address		
Phone		
Contact Person		
Dates Available		
Guest Capacity		
Rental Fee		
Time Allowed		
Overtime Charge		
Check Room		
PA System		
Air Conditioning		
Dance Floor		
Musical Instruments Available		
Cost		
Parking		
Food Available		
Cost Range		
Bar Facilities		
Cost Range		
Wedding Cake/Cost		
Decorations/Flowers		
Restrictions		
Linens		
Tableware		
Liability Insurance		
Gratuities		
Sales Tax		
Deposit Required		
Cancellation Fee		
Balance Due		
References		

CATERING ESTIMATES

	CATERER #1		CATERER #2	
Name				
Address				
Contact				
Phone				
MENU	#1	#2	#1	#2
Hors d'oeuvres				
Appetizers				
Soup				
Salad				
Main Course				
Side Dish				
Fruit				
Vegetable				
Cheeses				
Jello				
Bread/Rolls				
Beverages				
Desserts				
Nuts				
Wedding Cake				
Groom Cake				
Mints				
Misc.				
Cost/Person				
Cake-Cutting Fee				
Gratuities Included				
Required Deposit				
Cancellation Fee				
TOTALS				

Special Notes_____

_____

_____

_____

_____

_____

WEDDING PARTY STYLES

The Wedding Meal

BREAKFAST/BRUNCH
Average cost $15-35/person, including
      service and rentals
Features: Beverage, first course,
      main course, and dessert
Served between 9A.M.-11A.M.

LUNCHEONS
Average cost: $10-$65/person
All prices are inclusive
Features: Hors d'oeuvres, first
      course, main course,
      dessert, and beverage
Served between 12P.M.-3P.M.

COCKTAIL BUFFET
Average cost: $35-$50/person
Features: Hot and cold hors d'oeuvres,
      finger sandwiches, and
      wedding cake
Food can be served as a buffet or
      butler passed.
Served between 4P.M.-6P.M. or
      after 8P.M.

DINNER BUFFET
Average cost: $25-$100/person
Features: Hors d'oeuvres, appetizers,
      first course, main course,
      fresh fruits and vegetables,
      cheeses, bread, lavish desserts,
      and beverages served at food
      stations
Served between 5P.M.-8P.M.

SIT-DOWN DINNER
Average cost: $25-$100/person
Features: Very elegant setting and
      service of a full seven
      course meal.
Served between 5P.M.-8P.M.

DESSERT BUFFET
Average cost: $10/person
Features: A lavish sweet table with
      a variety of desserts and
      condiments. Champagne
      and/or coffee is included.
Served after 8P.M.

Our Menu

_____

_____

_____

_____

_____

_____

_____

Number of guests_____ Cost per person_____

TIPS ABOUT BEVERAGES

 • Offer both alcoholic and non-alcoholic beverages.

 • The "toasting" drink can be champagne, sparkling cider, bubbling punch, or white wine.

 • The general rule to follow is:
Each guest will consume two drinks in the first hour and one drink each hour following.
Children drink three glasses per hour.

 • The later in the day the reception is held the more guests will drink.

 • People drink white wine to red wine two to one.

WEDDING RECEPTION WITH 100-200 PEOPLE	
Dark and light liquors	50qt. bottles
Red and white wine	70qt. bottles
Champagne	70qt. bottles
Beer	5 barrels
Soda and drink mixes	70qt. bottles

 • Offer coffee near end of reception.

PARTY SUPPLIES LIST

Listed below are party supplies that you want to include:

ITEMS	NUMBER TO RENT	COST
1. Tables	_____	_____
2. Chairs	_____	_____
3. Table Linens	_____	_____
4. Wine Glasses	_____	_____
5. Bar Glasses	_____	_____
6. Champagne Glasses	_____	_____
7. China	_____	_____
8. Flatware	_____	_____
9. Serving Trays	_____	_____
10. Tents	_____	_____
11. Canopies	_____	_____
12. Lawn Umbrellas	_____	_____
13. Dancefloor	_____	_____
14. Bandstand	_____	_____
15. Extension Cords	_____	_____
16. Bars	_____	_____
17. Chafing Dishes	_____	_____
18. Coffee Urns	_____	_____
19. Punch Bowls	_____	_____
20. Candelabras	_____	_____
21. Coat Racks	_____	_____
22. Waiters	_____	_____
23. Wishing Wells	_____	_____
24. Table Skirting	_____	_____
25. Fountains	_____	_____
26.	_____	_____
27.	_____	_____

The Photographer

PHOTOGRAPHY ESTIMATES

Your wedding should be photographed by someone who understands just how special it is. Your portraits are the only permanent keepsake of you as a "bride." Because they cannot be changed or done over, it is important that a professional photographer with *wedding experience* capture those special moments.

Many professional photographers schedule wedding bookings up to one year in advance. They will also be happy to show you samples of their work and help you to select poses that flow from picture to picture creating a complete story.

Your photographer should be assigned to you for the entire day. Your coverage should include unlimited time and locations. He or she should also bring an extra camera system as a backup.

Use this comparison sheet for the selection of your photographer.

Estimate #1	Estimate #2
Name_____	Name_____
Address_____	Address_____
Phone_____	Phone_____
Appointment set for: _____	Appointment set for: _____
Contact_____	Contact_____
WEDDING PACKAGES offered:	WEDDING PACKAGES offered:
Description_____	Description_____
_____	_____
_____	_____
_____	_____
Prices_____	Prices_____
Size of prints_____	Size of prints_____
Number of prints_____	Number of prints_____
Number of proofs to choose from _____	Number of proofs to choose from _____
Additional prints (cost)_____	Additional prints (cost)_____
Travel costs_____	Travel costs_____
Album costs_____	Album costs_____
Payment plans_____	Payment plans_____
PORTRAITURE	*PORTRAITURE*
Engagement photo	Engagement photo
Cost_____ Deposit_____	Cost_____ Deposit_____
Bridal Portrait	Bridal Portrait
Cost_____ Deposit_____	Cost_____ Deposit_____
Glossies for Newspaper	Glossies for Newspaper
Cost_____ Deposit_____	Cost_____ Deposit_____
Date to view proofs_____	Date to view proofs_____
Special Notes	Special Notes
_____	_____
_____	_____

PHOTOGRAPHY CHOICES

There are three styles of photography which are available for your wedding album. They include: Portraiture, Candids, and "Special Effects" photography.

Your wedding photography will tell the exciting story of your wedding day. Mark the special poses from the lists below that you wish to include in your wedding story. Take this list with you when you meet with your photographer.

Portraiture is a planned pose of an individual or a group shot against a setting. A studio, chapel, or outdoor backdrops are usually used.

_____ Bride alone   _____ Bride and Attendants
_____ Bride and Groom standing   _____ Bride and Sisters
_____ Close-up of Bridal Couple   _____ Bride and Groom/Grandparents
_____ Bride and Parents   _____ Groom and Ushers
_____ Groom and Parents   _____ Groom and Brothers

Candids are photos of spontaneous events and activities which happen during the ceremony and reception.

_____ The Processional   _____ The Receiving Line
_____ Bride and Groom with Officiant   _____ Bride and Groom Toasting
_____ Bride and Groom Lighting   _____ Cutting the Cake
       Unity Candle   _____ Bride and Groom Eating Cake
_____ Exchanging of Rings   _____ Bride Throwing Bouquet
_____ The Bridal Kiss   _____ Guests Throwing Rice
_____ The Recessional   _____ Bride and Groom Driving Away
_____ Bride and Groom Arrival
       at Reception

Special Effects are stylized photographs that include close-ups, double exposures, "soft edge" focusing, and special filters. Also included are ethnic photos of family customs and traditions.

_____ The Food Table   _____ The Chapel
_____ The Wedding Cake   _____ Over the Threshold
_____ The Ring Pillow   _____ A Sixpence and a Bridal Shoe
_____ Hands and Wedding Rings   _____ The "Sweet Table"
_____ Champagne glasses/flowers   _____ Special Wedding Dances
_____ Special Customs in Action

Special Guests to Photograph:

_____

_____

_____

_____

_____

_____

_____

_____

_____

_____

_____

_____

_____

_____

_____

_____

_____

_____

_____

_____

_____

_____

_____

_____

_____

_____

_____

_____

_____

_____

_____

_____

_____

_____

_____

WEDDING VIDEOS

Tips about videotaping your wedding

Video provides a living moving memory of your wedding day. It is also an excellent way to share your day with relatives and friends who were unable to attend.

There are several styles of videos to choose from:

Nostalgic Video Incorporates other photos of the bridal couple as children or during the courtship and includes the honeymoon.
Approximate cost: $1000 or more

Documentary Video Uses only wedding day scenes. This style includes behind-the-scenes views of the bride getting ready, vows at the altar, guest interviews, and testimonials and anecdotes from family members and friends.
Approximate cost: $500-$700

Straight Shot Video Uses only one camera. Simple stills such as the names of the wedding couple and the wedding date are included with a musical introduction.
Approximate cost: $150-$300

Use this checklist to cover all of the videotaping details:

☐ Shop around.

☐ Get references.

☐ Ask to see demonstration tapes of each video style.

☐ Always request two cameras. One is used to focus specifically on the bride and groom. The other is to capture congregation reactions and the wedding recessional.

☐ Discuss restrictions at the ceremony site.

☐ Request videographer to attend rehearsal to determine placement of people and position of cameras.

☐ Inquire about liability insurance.

☐ Get a written contract.

☐ Include taping of bridal showers and bachelor parties, as well as the rehearsal dinner.

Special Notes About This Month's Details

Month of: _____

SUNDAY	MONDAY	TUESDAY	WEDNESDAY	THURSDAY	FRIDAY	SATURDAY
____	____	____	____	____	____	____
____	____	____	____	____	____	____
____	____	____	____	____	____	____
____	____	____	____	____	____	____
____	____	____	____	____	____	____

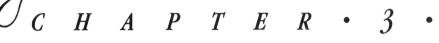

C H A P T E R · 3 ·

MONTHS BEFORE

Wedding Gown Guidelines

·

Bridesmaids' Attire

·

Formal Wear

·

Parents' Responsibilities

 *My* Wedding Gown

WHAT I WANT TO LOOK LIKE:

On this page, sketch or attach a bridal magazine picture of the gown you want to wear on your wedding day. This will help you in coordinating your bridal bouquet, matching bridesmaids gowns, and choosing appropriate formal wear.

WEDDING GOWNS I LIKE:

#1 Description _____

_____

_____

_____

Manufacturer _____

Model # _____ Cost _____

Store _____ Phone _____

Contact _____

_____

#2 Description _____

_____

_____

_____

Manufacturer _____

Model # _____ Cost _____

Store _____ Phone _____

Contact _____

_____

#3 Description _____

_____

_____

_____

Manufacturer _____

Model # _____ Cost _____

Store _____ Phone _____

Contact _____

_____

Tips about buying the gown

- ☐ Shop five to six months before the wedding.
- ☐ Stores carry "samples" only—gown must be special ordered.
- ☐ A deposit of one third of the cost will be required.
- ☐ Be prepared—wear shoes and undergarments you expect to wear on your wedding day.
- ☐ When gown arrives, a "fitting" will be arranged.
- ☐ All special alterations are charged as extra!
- ☐ Check the store's exchange and cancellation policy before you order.
- ☐ Keep all receipts.
- ☐ *Everything should be in writing—including the delivery date.*
- ☐ Coordinate your accessories—gloves, handbag, etc.
- ☐ Pick up gown as close to wedding day as possible.
- ☐ Ask for ironing instructions, or ask about pressing charges.
- ☐ At home, hang gown on a door and spread train so it won't wrinkle.
- ☐ Your veil and headpiece are separate items and separate charges.
- ☐ Consider a detachable veil.
- ☐ Try on headpieces while wearing gown.
- ☐ Wear your engagement ring on your right hand during your ceremony. Afterward, place it in front of your wedding ring.

Details about my wedding day attire

Bridal Shop_____

Address_____

Contact Person_____ Phone_____

Details:	**Costs:**
Wedding Gown_____	_____
Manufacturer_____	
Tag #_____	
Headpiece_____	_____
Manufacturer_____	
Tag #_____	
Veil_____	_____
Manufacturer_____	
Tag #_____	
Accessories:_____	
Shoes_____	_____
Hosiery_____	_____
Slip_____	_____
Bra_____	_____
Gloves_____	_____
Jewelry_____	_____
Other_____	_____
TOTAL COST	

Alterations:

Fitting dates/times   1st_____ · 2nd_____

Costs_____

Delivery Date_____

NOTES

_____

_____

_____

Bridesmaids' Attire

On this page, sketch or attach a photo from a bridal magazine of the dresses you are considering for your bridesmaids to wear. (This will help you in selecting coordinating bouquets and accessories for them.)

DRESSES TO CONSIDER:

#1 Dress Choice _____

Description _____
_____
_____

Headpiece _____
Manufacturer _____
Model # _____ Cost _____
Store _____ Phone _____
Contact _____

#2 Dress Choice _____

Description _____
_____
_____

Headpiece _____
Manufacturer _____
Model # _____ Cost _____
Store _____ Phone _____
Contact _____

#3 Dress Choice _____

Description _____
_____
_____

Headpiece _____
Manufacturer _____
Model # _____ Cost _____
Store _____ Phone _____
Contact _____

Tips about buying bridesmaids dresses

☐ Dresses should be the same length and formality as bride's gown.

☐ Make sure dress flatters a variety of figures and can be worn again.

☐ Accessories should be simple.

☐ Choose a color according to the season.

☐ Shoes and stockings should match or be coordinated to the dresses.

☐ Keep within the bridesmaids' budgets.

☐ Bridesmaids dresses do NOT have to be identical.

☐ Junior Bridesmaids may match or blend with maids dresses. Best ages are ten to sixteen years.

☐ Flower girls wear a long or short dress that matches or compliments others. Best ages are four to nine years.

☐ Bridesmaids dresses usually require some alterations.

☐ Order all of the dresses at the same time in order to avoid color variations.

Accessories	Cost
◆ Headpiece	
◆ Shoes	
◆ Hosiery	
◆ Gloves	
◆ Handbag	
◆ Jewelry	

BRIDE'S ATTENDANTS LIST

Maid/Matron of Honor _____

Address _____ Phone _____

City _____ State _____ Zip _____

Sizes: Dress _____ Shoe _____ Hose _____ Glove _____ Head _____

Bridesmaid _____

Address _____ Phone _____

City _____ State _____ Zip _____

Sizes: Dress _____ Shoe _____ Hose _____ Glove _____ Head _____

Bridesmaid _____

Address _____ Phone _____

City _____ State _____ Zip _____

Sizes: Dress _____ Shoe _____ Hose _____ Glove _____ Head _____

Bridesmaid _____

Address _____ Phone _____

City _____ State _____ Zip _____

Sizes: Dress _____ Shoe _____ Hose _____ Glove _____ Head _____

Bridesmaid _____

Address _____ Phone _____

City _____ State _____ Zip _____

Sizes: Dress _____ Shoe _____ Hose _____ Glove _____ Head _____

Bridesmaid _____

Address _____ Phone _____

City _____ State _____ Zip _____

Sizes: Dress _____ Shoe _____ Hose _____ Glove _____ Head _____

Bridesmaid/Flower Girl _____

Address _____ Phone _____

City _____ State _____ Zip _____

Sizes: Dress _____ Shoe _____ Hose _____ Glove _____ Head _____

Formal Wear

TUXEDO STYLES

Six classic styles that always fit the occasion

FORMAL FULL-DRESS TUXEDO

"The Avanti"
FORMAL FULL-DRESS WHITE
The General Rule is:
When the weather outside is
warmer than the weather inside...
The groom wears white!

46

"The Wedding Tuxedo"
CLASSIC CUTAWAY TUXEDO

"The Starlight"
AFTER SIX STAR COLLECTION
The classic tuxedo with
matching vest and bow tie.

"The Galaxy"
AFTER SIX STAR COLLECTION
Formal black dinner jacket
with matching trousers.

"The Gemini"
AFTER SIX STAR COLLECTION
Formal white dinner
jacket with black trousers
and bow tie.

ESTIMATES FOR FORMAL WEAR

	Store #1		Store #2	
	Name		Name	
	Phone		Phone	
		Cost		Cost
Groom				
Style				
Color				
Attendants				
Style				
Color				
Fathers				
Style				
Color				
Child Attendants				
Shoes				
Accessories				
Misc.				
TOTAL COST				
Deposit				
Fitting Date				
Return Date				
Return Date				

GROOM'S ATTENDANTS LIST

Best Man _____

Address _____ Phone _____

City _____ State _____ Zip _____

Sizes: Sleeve _____ Neck _____ Waist _____ Trouser Inseam _____ Shoe _____

Head Usher _____

Address _____ Phone _____

City _____ State _____ Zip _____

Sizes: Sleeve _____ Neck _____ Waist _____ Trouser Inseam _____ Shoe _____

Usher _____

Address _____ Phone _____

City _____ State _____ Zip _____

Sizes: Sleeve _____ Neck _____ Waist _____ Trouser Inseam _____ Shoe _____

Usher _____

Address _____ Phone _____

City _____ State _____ Zip _____

Sizes: Sleeve _____ Neck _____ Waist _____ Trouser Inseam _____ Shoe _____

Usher _____

Address _____ Phone _____

City _____ State _____ Zip _____

Sizes: Sleeve _____ Neck _____ Waist _____ Trouser Inseam _____ Shoe _____

Usher _____

Address _____ Phone _____

City _____ State _____ Zip _____

Sizes: Sleeve _____ Neck _____ Waist _____ Trouser Inseam _____ Shoe _____

Usher/Ring Bearer _____

Address _____ Phone _____

City _____ State _____ Zip _____

Sizes: Sleeve _____ Neck _____ Waist _____ Trouser Inseam _____ Shoe _____

*C*hecklist of Parents' Responsibilities

Do's and Dont's for Divorced Parents

Item	Duties	Performed By
Engagement	Host and engagement party. Officially announce engagement and wedding date. Invite groom's parents to meet and discuss wedding plans.	Bride's parents or parent with whom the bride lives.
The Guest List	Provide complete list of family and friends as promptly as possible	Mothers
Invitations Newspaper Announcement	Person named on wedding invitation	Parent who is "hosting" wedding
Rehearsal Dinner	Host the dinner party	Groom's parents
	Attend party	All parents
Gift-Opening Party	Host party, usually held in a private home the day following the wedding	Either parent
Receiving Line	Stand in line and greet guests as they enter. Introduce bride and groom to distant relatives and friends.	Mothers
	Mingle among guests	Fathers, stepparents
Ceremony	Read special poems or passages. Act as best man or matron of honor. Escort bride down the aisle.	Any parents
Ceremony Seating (divorced parents)	Seated in Row #1 Seated in Row #3	Parent who raised bride. Other parent and their new spouse or escort.
Reception	Hosting of individual tables.	All parents

continued . . .

Item	Duties	Performed By
Photographs	Picture taking together or with family groups	Individual decisions based on what works best
Wedding Dance	Join in wedding dance	Parents dance with spouses or another family member
Wedding Rehearsal	Arrive on time to practice their part in wedding ceremony.	All parents
Wedding Gift	Financial circumstances dictate the generosity of the gift. Any gift is correct.	All parents

Whether your parents are divorced or not, this is *your* wedding day, and all parents concerned should be willing to cooperate to make the day enjoyable. Be sensitive to your parents' feelings. Make it known that their presence is important to you. Do everything to keep a comfortable distance between divorced parents. If someone is stubborn, tell them that their presence will be missed and that you hope they will change their mind. Then leave them alone to decide.

Special Notes About This Month's Details

Month of: _____

SUNDAY	MONDAY	TUESDAY	WEDNESDAY	THURSDAY	FRIDAY	SATURDAY
____	____	____	____	____	____	____
____	____	____	____	____	____	____
____	____	____	____	____	____	____
____	____	____	____	____	____	____
____	____	____	____	____	____	____

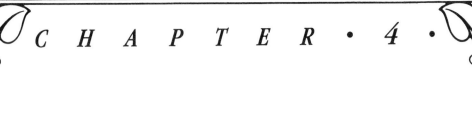

REMARRIAGE
PLANNING

Ceremony and Reception Etiquette

·

Children in the Wedding

Remarriage Planning

REMARRIAGE GUIDELINES

Today in forty-three percent of all marrying couples, at least one partner is divorced. Remarriage, often referred to as an "encore" wedding, is guided by one rule: The wedding should suit your age and lifestyle.

Consider the following etiquette guidelines in planning your remarriage ceremony and reception:

Your Engagement

Tell the children first. Next, tell all parents. Finally tell your friends and relatives.

An engagement ring is appropriate.

A newspaper announcement of your engagement is acceptable.

Kinds of Weddings

Civil and nonsectarian ceremonies are most popular.

A traditional wedding is proper if the bride has never been married before.

A judge or magistrate can officiate at a ceremony wherever it is held.

Consult a clergy member if a church wedding is desired.

Who Is Invited

Family members and close friends are usually invited.

Telephone invitations may be used. Personal handwritten notes are acceptable.

Fifty or more guests require a printed invitation.

Ex-spouses are usually not included on the guest list.

Widowed persons may invite former in-laws.

Pre-Wedding Parties

Bridal showers are appropriate.

Wedding gifts are not required.

Written thank-you notes must be sent for all gifts received.

Wedding Attire

The bride can wear white or any other color she chooses.

The groom may choose either a tuxedo or a dress suit.

A floor length bridal gown is the accepted length limit. No trains.

A hat or hair ornament replaces veil.

Wedding Traditions

Bride may be escorted down the aisle or walk alone.

A receiving line is proper.

A wedding cake should be included.

Throwing the bouquet is optional.

A wedding toast is appropriate.

Photographs and flowers are included.

Only honor attendants are required.

The remarriage couple pays for their own wedding.

A parent's offer to contribute should be accepted.

CHILDREN IN THE WEDDING

Include your children in your remarriage in every way possible. Creating an event in which all of the children play an important part helps to establish a "blended" family right from the start.

Some ideas for children's roles in the wedding are:

The children may serve as attendants in the bridal party.

The children may escort Mom down the aisle.

A girl or boy may distribute mass books or wedding programs.

A child may be in charge of the guest book.

A child may pass out rice packets.

A child may read scripture passages during the ceremony.

Children may help in preparing invitations.

Children may help to decorate the reception hall and wedding cards.

An older child may transport wedding gifts to the home after the wedding.

An older child may be in charge of the storage of the top layer of the wedding cake.

All of the children may be included in a Unity Candle lighting segment in the wedding ceremony. During this special "ceremony within the ceremony," each family member holds a lighted candle. The bride and groom then light one central candle with their two lighted tapers to symbolize the joining of their two families. There are many variations of this family candle lighting ceremony, and all should be planned with the clergy member who will be officiating.

Special Notes About This Month's Details

Month of: _____

SUNDAY	MONDAY	TUESDAY	WEDNESDAY	THURSDAY	FRIDAY	SATURDAY

CHAPTER · 5 ·

7

MONTHS BEFORE

The Florist

•

Wedding Gift Registry

•

The Honeymoon Arrangements

FLORAL CHECKLIST

☐ Look at samples and floral catalogues.

☐ Bring along color swatches of the dress fabric.

☐ Check to see if any attendant is allergic to certain flowers.

☐ A bridal bouquet may be any color.

☐ The bridal bouquet is usually proportional to the height of the bride.

☐ Attendants' bouquets should harmonize with their gowns.

☐ The honor attendant's bouquet may be larger or a different color if desired.

☐ Boutonnieres are generally white in color.

☐ The groom's boutonniere is different from the groomsmen's.

☐ Ask the florist if they preserve the bouquets.

☐ The length of the aisle carpet needed for your church is_____ feet.

☐ Ask about delivery and set-up charges.

☐ Be sure to have flowers delivered early enough if photos will be taken before the ceremony.

☐ Send a bouquet of flowers to each set of parents one day after the wedding as a special thank-you.

WEDDING BOUQUET "TIPS"

Always include your favorite flower in your wedding bouquet — it will bring you good luck.

Traditionally, the groom's boutonniere is one of the flowers from the bride's bouquet.

As you walk down the aisle, hold your wedding bouquet no higher than your waistline.

To keep the bouquet upright and fully displayed, hold the stem of the bouquet between your pointer and index fingers, instead of grasping it with your full hand.

The Florist

Our Floral Plan
(copy should be given to the florist)

PERSONAL FLOWERS

Quantity	Person	Description
	Bride:	
	Bouquet	
	Toss bouquet (optional)	
	Going away corsage	
	Bridesmaids:	
	Honor attendant	
	Bridesmaids	
	Flower girl	
	Groom and Attendants:	
	Groom's boutonniere	
	Ushers' boutonnieres	
	Parents/Relatives:	
	Mother of the bride	
	Mother of the groom	
	Grandmothers	
	Other Relatives:	
	Father of the bride	
	Father of the groom	
	Other relatives	

Our Floral Plan

CEREMONY FLOWERS

Quantity	Item	Description
	Arch/Canopy	(color/size/type)
	Kneeler	
	Candelabra	
	White candles	
	Floral sprays	
	Potted flowers	
	Pew decorations	
	Aisle ribbons	
	Aisle carpet (length_____)	
	Other	

Special Notes

_____

_____

_____

_____

_____

_____

_____

_____

RECEPTION FLOWERS

Quantity	Item	Description
		(color/size/type)
	Table centerpieces	
	Bride's table	
	Parents' tables	
	Guests' tables	
	Other:	
	Table garlands	
	Top of cake	
	Cake table	
	Guest book stand	
	Other	

Staple color
swatch here:

Ceremony Site _____

Address _____

Delivery Time _____

Reception Site _____

Address _____

Contact Person _____

Delivery Time _____

FLORIST ESTIMATES

Estimate #1	Estimate #2
Name_____	Name_____
Address_____	Address_____
Phone_____	Phone_____
Contact_____	Contact_____
PERSONAL FLOWERS COST	**PERSONAL FLOWERS** COST
Bride's bouquet	Bride's bouquet
Throw away	Throw away
Bridesmaids (each)	Bridesmaids (each)
Flower girl	Flower girl
Bride's mother	Bride's mother
Groom's mother	Groom's mother
Grandmothers	Grandmothers
Godmothers	Godmothers
Aunts	Aunts
Groom's boutonniere	Groom's boutonniere
Boutonnieres (each)	Boutonnieres (each)
CEREMONY FLOWERS Altar flowers	**CEREMONY FLOWERS** Altar flowers
Candelabras/candles	Candelabras/candles
Pew decorations	Pew decorations
Kneeler	Kneeler
Aisle ribbons	Aisle ribbons
Cloth aisle runner	Cloth aisle runner
RECEPTION FLOWERS Head table	**RECEPTION FLOWERS** Head table
Centerpieces	Centerpieces
Other	Other
Delivery charge	Delivery charge
Set-up charge	Set-up charge
TOTAL COST	TOTAL COST
Deposit	Deposit
Balance Due	Balance Due

Wedding Gift Registry

Gift Registry Guidelines

The bridal registry is actually a listing of all the gifts that you would like to receive. The store that has your list will show it to anyone who asks to see it. As items are purchased, they are removed from the list so that duplications do not occur.

When making your wedding gift "wish" list, keep the following important facts in mind:

• Shop with your groom so that you make choices together.

• List all pattern numbers and color choices.

• Consider registering at two stores to give wider price choice to your guests.

• Inform your family and friends where you have registered.

• Discuss return policies with the bridal registrar.

• Most bridal registries will provide you with a free preprinted listing of gift and household items they offer.

• Most stores that have a bridal registry offer a computerized listing service that is interconnected with all of their locations.

• Encourage guests to send gifts directly to your home rather than bring them to the reception.

• Don't open any gifts at the reception.

• Inquire about a temporary insurance policy that will cover all gifts during the time that they are being displayed in your home before the wedding.

• Assign a friend to safely transport all gifts from the reception site to your home.

• If the wedding is temporarily postponed, all gifts are kept.

• If the wedding is cancelled, all gifts must be returned with a note of explanation.

As Gifts Arrive:

+ Open each gift immediately and carefully.

+ Record the gift as soon as it is received, or tape the card to the gift until you record it.

+ If the gift arrives broken or damaged, immediately call or write the store where it was purchased.

+ Do not return or exchange anything before the wedding, especially if you are planning to display your gifts.

+ Exchange gifts only if the giver will not learn of it.

Wedding Gift Listings

On these pages, record all wrapped gifts received. Include dates that thank-you notes were sent out. All cards and envelopes should be kept together. Write amount of monetary gift inside of each card. Also note that thank-you was sent out.

Name Address City, State, Zip	Shower gift	Thank you	Date Sent	Wedding gift	Thank you	Date Sent

Name Address City, State, Zip	Shower gift	Thank you	Date Sent	Wedding gift	Thank you	Date Sent

Name Address City, State, Zip	Shower gift	Thank you	Date Sent	Wedding gift	Thank you	Date Sent

$\mathcal{T}$he Honeymoon Arrangements

The Travel Accommodations

Travel Agency _____

Address _____

Agent _____

Phone _____

Honeymoon Dates From _____ To _____

Travel Reservations

Date	Carrier	Departs	Arrives	Cost

Rental Car

Date	Agency		Cost

Hotel Reservations

Hotel _____

Address _____

Contact Person _____ Phone _____

Room Description _____ Room # _____

Rate _____ Reservation: ☐ Made ☐ Confirmed

Arrival Date _____ Departure Date _____

Packing for the Honeymoon

List all the items you want to take with you on your honeymoon trip here:

BE SURE TO BRING:

☐ Your drivers license

☐ Proof of age/citizenship (birth certificate)

☐ Marriage license

☐ Passport or visa

☐ Names, addresses, and phone numbers of all parents

☐ Your doctor's name and telephone number

☐ Copies of your regular prescriptions

☐ List of credit card numbers

☐ Checking account number

☐ Shopping list with everyone's sizes

☐ List of recommended restaurants and tourist attractions

☐ List of luggage contents (for any loss claims)

☐ The name and phone number of your local drug store for prescription refills

☐ Bring plastic bags for wet bathing suits and extra toiletries

☐ Don't forget your camera and several extra rolls of film

Clothing	Toiletries
Lingerie	Toothbrush
	Shampoo
	First Aid kit

Equipment	Don't Forget to:
Camera	Stop Mail
Address Book	Set Light Timers
	Get Pet Feeder

Special Notes About This Month's Details

Month of: _____

SUNDAY	MONDAY	TUESDAY	WEDNESDAY	THURSDAY	FRIDAY	SATURDAY

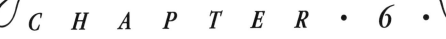

C H A P T E R · 6 ·

MONTHS BEFORE

Wedding Stationery

·

The Wedding Cake

THE INVITATION CHECKLIST

Follow these guidelines to prepare your invitations properly.

- Make an appointment to look at samples.

- Discuss particular etiquette and wording.

- Ask to receive envelopes earlier to begin addressing them. Order extras in case of mistakes.

- Handwrite all invitations—never typewrite an address.

- Any color ink may be used.

- Request a proof of the invitation before it is printed.

- Check for typographical and spelling errors.

- Mail invitations six weeks before the wedding. Holiday weddings should allow eight weeks.

- A standard invitation weighs two ounces and *requires two stamps*.

- Take a completed invitation to the post office to check its exact weight.

NOTE! The post office now REQUIRES the return address to be printed in the upper left-hand corner of the envelope.

How Many Invitations Do You Need?

- One invitation should be sent to every married couple (including officiant and his wife).

- Each single adult guest, even if they are living with their parents.

- Each attendant and their parents.

- Everyone in the groom's immediate family.

- Extras for families as keepsakes.

Wedding Stationery

Stationery items to know

THE ITEM	WHAT IT IS FOR
Engagement Announcement	This notice, printed in a formal wedding invitation format, announces that you are officially engaged.
Wedding Invitations and Envelopes	This notice can be printed or engraved. It is sent to anyone you want to attend the wedding ceremony. This notice gives full information about the event.
Pew Cards	These specially printed cards are used to mark reserved seating at the wedding ceremony.
Reception Cards	This card, placed inside of the wedding invitation, announces the time and place of the reception.
Response Card and Envelope	A printed card placed inside of the wedding invitation along with a stamped, self-addressed envelope. This card is to be returned with a number indicating how many people will be attending your ceremony and/or reception.
Wedding Announcements	This printed card, which formally announces your change in status, is sent, after your wedding, to all of the people who were not invited to attend.
At Home Cards	A printed card that lists your complete new address.
Thank-You Formals	A special card on which a personal thank-you message can be handwritten for all gifts received from your marriage.
Informals	This stationery is used for all personal notes and correspondence that are written after your marriage. Your married name is usually imprinted on the outside cover.

STATIONERY ESTIMATES

Estimate #1	Estimate #2
Name_____	Name_____
Address_____	Address_____
Phone_____	Phone_____
Contact_____	Contact_____
Invitations_____ Style #_____	Invitations_____ Style #_____
Number needed_____	Number needed_____
Paper color_____	Paper color_____
Paper stock_____	Paper stock_____
Type style_____	Type style_____
Ink color_____ Cost_____	Ink color_____ Cost_____
Reception Cards_____ Style #_____	Reception Cards_____ Style #_____
Number needed_____ Cost_____	Number needed_____ Cost_____
Response Cards_____ Style #_____	Response Cards_____ Style #_____
Number needed_____ Cost_____	Number needed_____ Cost_____
Thank-you notes_____ Style #_____	Thank-you notes_____ Style #_____
Number needed_____ Cost_____	Number needed_____ Cost_____
Announcement_____ Style #_____	Announcement_____ Style #_____
Number needed_____ Cost_____	Number needed_____ Cost_____
Wedding Favors_____ Style #_____	Wedding Favors_____ Style #_____
Number needed_____ Cost_____	Number needed_____ Cost_____
Matches_____ Style #_____	Matches_____ Style #_____
Number needed_____ Cost_____	Number needed_____ Cost_____
TOTAL COST_____	TOTAL COST_____
Deposit_____	Deposit_____
Balance due when_____	Balance due when_____
Terms of Cancellation_____ (if order is not produced correctly)	Terms of Cancellation_____ (if order is not produced correctly)

LOCATION MAPS

Number of copies needed_____

Type of paper_____

Color ink_____

Cost_____

Draw the map details in pencil. When you have completed the drawing, trace over the pencil with black ink or marker. The drawing can be duplicated at any instant printer.

To Ceremony Site

To Reception Site

PROPER ADDRESSING

♦ Always write out all names and words in full. Abbreviations are not permitted except for "Mrs.," "Mr.," "Messrs.," "Dr.," and "Jr."

♦ No symbols are allowed—write out the word "and."

GUEST	INNER ENVELOPE	OUTER ENVELOPE
Husband and wife	Mr. and Mrs. Smith	Mr. and Mrs. John Smith
Never write "and family." Children under sixteen should be listed in the inner envelope only.		
Husband, wife, and children under sixteen	Mr. and Mrs. Smith David, Susan, and James (in order of age)	Mr. and Mrs. John Smith
Children over sixteen should receive a separate invitation.		
Two sisters over eighteen still at home	The Misses Smith	The Misses Sue and Mary Smith
Two brothers over sixteen still at home	The Messrs. Black	The Messrs. James and Charles Black
Married but wife has kept maiden name	Ms. Johnson Mr. Smith	Ms. Mary Johnson Mr. John Smith
Single woman	Miss Downs	Miss Susan Downs
Single woman and guest	Miss Downs and Guest	Miss Mary Downs
Single man and guest	Mr. Lang and Guest	Mr. Edward Lang
Engaged couple	Mr. Martin and Miss Wallace	Mr. Glenn Martin
Widow	Mrs. Green	Mrs. Steven Green
Unmarried couple living together	Miss Matthew Mr. Hale	Miss Joan Matthew Mr. Robert Hale
Divorcée	Mrs. Grant	Mrs. Mary Grant

Invitation Assembly

After all of the envelopes have been addressed, place the enclosures into the inner envelope in this manner:

• The reception card is placed inside of the invitation.

• Place the map (if used) inside of the invitation.

• Place the response card in its envelope.

• Put a stamp on the envelope and place it inside of the invitation.

1. All of the above enclosures should then be placed inside of the inner envelope facing the back flap.

2. Place the inner envelope with its front facing the back of the outer envelope.

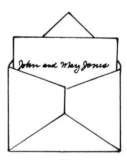

Return address must be placed in the upper left corner of the front of the outer envelope.

3.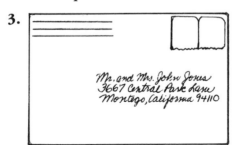

Two stamps (usually necessary)

All addresses should be hand-written. The only figures that should be used are the street numbers and zip codes.

82

The Wedding Cake

Wedding Cake Guidelines

• Look at photos of baker's previous work.

• Compare costs and workmanship.

• Taste test the cake and frosting.

• A wedding cake can be any size or shape.

• A wedding cake includes the wedding colors.

• Cake flavor is no longer limited to white cake. Banana, cheesecake, chocolate, or carrot are among the top choices.

• Discuss delivery and set-up of the cake.

• Frosting and ornamentation may be as elaborate as you desire.

• The cake should be displayed on its own decorated table at the reception site.

• The top layer of the wedding cake should be removed and frozen for the first wedding anniversary.

• The groom's cake is a smaller cake baked in any creative shape. It is usually decorated to depict the groom's occupation or favorite hobby, and is delivered and displayed next to the wedding cake at the reception.

Photo or sketch of cake I like.

Photo or sketch of groom's cake I want.

CAKE ESTIMATES

Estimate #1	Estimate #2
Name_____	Name_____
Address_____	Address_____
Contact_____	Contact_____
Phone_____	Phone_____
Cake Description_____	Cake Description_____
_____	_____
_____	_____
Size of cake_____	Size of cake_____
Number of layers_____	Number of layers_____
Number of servings_____	Number of servings_____
Shape_____	Shape_____
Cake flavor_____	Cake flavor_____
Filling_____	Filling_____
Icing_____	Icing_____
Colors_____	Colors_____
Ornament_____	Ornament_____
Cost_____	Cost_____
Groom's Cake	*Groom's Cake*
Description_____	Description_____
_____	_____
_____	_____
Cost_____	Cost_____
Extra Costs	*Extra Costs*
Cutting and Serving Fee_____	Cutting and Serving Fee_____
Delivery and Set-up_____	Delivery and Set-up_____
Total cost_____	Total cost_____
Deposit_____	Deposit_____
Balance due_____	Balance due_____

Special Notes About This Month's Details

Month of: _____

SUNDAY	MONDAY	TUESDAY	WEDNESDAY	THURSDAY	FRIDAY	SATURDAY
_____	_____	_____	_____	_____	_____	_____
_____	_____	_____	_____	_____	_____	_____
_____	_____	_____	_____	_____	_____	_____
_____	_____	_____	_____	_____	_____	_____
_____	_____	_____	_____	_____	_____	_____

C H A P T E R · 7 ·

MONTHS BEFORE

Music for the Wedding

·

Ceremony Programs

·

Reception Entertainment

·

Wedding Decorations

Music for the Wedding

Special notes to guide you when selecting the musical entertainment for your wedding.

1. Shop around and compare prices and packages offered.

2. Consider an agency. They offer videos of all their bands. This is a unique way to see many bands at one time.

3. Call every band you are considering. During the call, be sure to:

- Discuss the band's fee.

- Discuss any overtime fees.

- Ask about "auditioning" the band at another wedding.

- Inquire about the band leader's willingness to announce reception activities.

- Inquire about a vocalist with the band.

- Ask for references.

4. Once you have decided which band you want, meet with the band leader. Ask about:

- Song choices. Select songs that will appeal to a wide range of musical tastes.

- Discuss breaks during the reception. How many? How long?

- Does the band play special requests?

- Discuss how you want them to dress.

- Put all arrangements *in writing*.

- Be prepared to make a deposit at the time of booking.

- The balance of the fee will be required at the end of the reception.

5. The average band's performance time is four hours. It is *not* necessary to "tip" the band.

6. Most deejay bands charge between $250 and $500 for a four hour performance of continuous music. (Add $100 for a light show.)

7. Most live bands charge between $450-$7000 for a four hour performance. Overtime fees range from $25-$100 per musician per hour.

MUSIC ESTIMATES

Live Band #1	Disc Jockey #1
Name_____	Name_____
Phone_____	Phone_____
Size of Band_____	Size of Band_____
Includes: _____	Includes: _____
_____	_____
_____	_____
Cost:_____	Cost:_____

Live Band #2	Disc Jockey #2
Name_____	Name_____
Phone_____	Phone_____
Size of Band_____	Size of Band_____
Includes: _____	Includes: _____
_____	_____
_____	_____
Cost:_____	Cost:_____

Live Band #3	Disc Jockey #3
Name_____	Name_____
Phone_____	Phone_____
Size of Band_____	Size of Band_____
Includes: _____	Includes: _____
_____	_____
_____	_____
Cost:_____	Cost:_____

Special Notes_____
_____
_____
_____
_____
_____

WEDDING PROGRAMS

The wedding program is a printed listing of the details of your wedding ceremony. It is usually printed on an 8½″ x 11″ sheet of paper that is folded in half to form 1) a front cover; 2) a centerfold; 3) a back cover.

I. *THE FRONT COVER* is the title page and includes the following:

- A DESCRIPTIVE PHRASE EXAMPLE (Welcome to the Marriage Ceremony of)
- BRIDE'S NAME
- GROOM'S NAME

- DAY AND DATE
- TIME
- CEREMONY LOCATION
- CITY AND STATE

II. *THE CENTERFOLD* pages contain:

A. *The Order of Service*, which outlines the individual segments of the service.

SEGMENT	SONG/PASSAGE SELECTED	SUNG/READ/PLAYED BY
Prelude		
Seating of Parents		
First Solo		
Processional		
Scripture Readings		
Lighting of Unity Candle		
Offertory		
Communion		
Recessional		
Postlude		

B. *The Participants* in the wedding ceremony

Officiant _____

Parents of the bride _____

Parents of the groom _____

Grandparents _____

Grandparents _____

Maid of Honor . . . . Name _____

Relationship _____

Best Man . . . . Name _____

Relationship _____

Bridesmaids	Groomsmen
Name_____	Name_____
Relationship_____	Relationship_____
Name_____	Name_____
Relationship_____	Relationship_____
Name_____	Name_____
Relationship_____	Relationship_____
Name_____	Name_____
Relationship_____	Relationship_____

Readers . . . . Name _____

Relationship _____

Name _____

Relationship _____

Name _____

Relationship _____

Gift Bearers . . . . Name _____

Relationship _____

Name _____

Relationship _____

Organist . . . . Name _____

Soloist . . . . Name _____

III. *THE BACK COVER* offers a place to print a short personal message or expression of thanks to your guests.

Special notations about the reception, picture taking, or any other necessary information for your guests can also be printed here.

EXAMPLE:

TO OUR WEDDING GUESTS
On this day which marks the beginning of
our lives together, your presence here is
important to us and greatly appreciated.
We hope that you will continue to be a part
of our lives. Without friends, family, and
parents, we have very little.

THE RECEPTION PROGRAM

This form will enable the band leader to properly introduce your bridal party and other important people who will be a part of your reception program. Fill out each name and song selection. Make a copy of this form and give it to your band leader before the wedding, so that he will be able to announce all of the people involved.

Activity	Time scheduled	People Involved	Song to be played
Bridal Party Arrives			
Receiving Line			
Grace to be said			
Toast to be made			
During Meal			
First Dance (Your Favorite Song)		Bride and Groom:	
		Bride's Parents:	
		Groom's Parents:	
		Maid of Honor	
		Best Man	
		Flower Girl	
		Ring Bearer	
Cake Cutting			
Bouquet Toss			
Garter Throw			
Special Ethnic Dances			
Last Dance			

Decorations and Accessories

Suggestions for decorative accessories that can be purchased or rented to add a festive atmosphere to your wedding site.

ACCESSORIES	BALLOONS
Floral decorations on the head table Floral decorations on the guests' tables Ice sculptures Fountains Candles Balloons Colored lights Mirrored table centers Napkin rings Illuminated dancefloors A lighted marquee Live decorated trees A wishing well box for envelope gifts Keepsake champagne glasses engraved with names and date Packets of bird seed, rose petals, or confetti to throw Individually wrapped candy favors for wedding guests	Balloons have become the most popular form of decoration used for wedding sites today. Balloon professionals offer numerous decorative ideas and designs. Request to see their portfolio of previous work to see the quality of their work. Some balloon decorations to consider: • balloon arches • balloon centerpieces • balloon release (a symbolic celebration of new life) • a balloon heart • balloon pew markers • balloons and flowers used as altar decorations

Your wedding "color" can be used for:

The bridesmaids' dresses   Table centerpieces
Table linens/napkins   Wedding favors
Room decorations   Floral bouquets
Altar decorations   Invitations

Special Notes About This Month's Details

Month of: _____

SUNDAY	MONDAY	TUESDAY	WEDNESDAY	THURSDAY	FRIDAY	SATURDAY

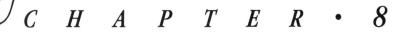

C H A P T E R • *8* •

MONTHS BEFORE

Bridal Party Limousines

•

Wedding Day Transportation

•

Out-of-Town Guests

•

Attendants' Gifts

•

Pre-Wedding Parties

Transportation

BRIDAL PARTY LIMOUSINE ESTIMATES

A chauffer-driven limousine is one of the most fashionable modes of travel used for special occasions. If you are considering one, follow these guidelines:

☐ A "stretch" limousine is the standard type of vehicle used for weddings. It includes a variety of luxuries.

☐ Limousine rates range between $25 to $150 per hour. A minimum of three hours of rental time is usually required.

☐ Reservations are necessary. Make them at least three months in advance of the wedding date.

☐ A deposit of fifty percent is required with the reservation. The balance is due and paid at the time of pickup.

☐ Be sure to ask about the company's cancellation policy.

☐ If you borrow a friend's or relative's car, be sure to offer to have the car washed, and thank the owner with a small gift and a full tank of gas.

☐ Carriages or other special vehicles may require a permit. Check with the local police station about any restrictions.

ESTIMATE #1

Company Name_____

Phone_____

Contact_____

Type of vehicle_____

Vehicle holds_____people

Rental includes:

_____

_____

_____

_____

Rate_____

Overtime rate_____

Cancellation_____

Deposit_____

Balance due_____

ESTIMATE #2

Company Name_____

Phone_____

Contact_____

Type of vehicle_____

Vehicle holds_____people

Rental includes:

_____

_____

_____

_____

Rate_____

Overtime rate_____

Cancellation_____

Deposit_____

Balance due_____

WEDDING DAY TRANSPORTATION

If you will be providing transportation for out-of-town guests on your wedding day, use this list to coordinate trips. (A copy should be given to each driver.)

GUEST	PICK-UP LOCATION	PICK-UP TIME	PHONE

Ceremony Address _____

Time of Ceremony _____

Directions:

_____

_____

_____

Reception Address _____

Reception time _____

Directions:

_____

_____

_____

OUT-OF-TOWN GUESTS

All special long-distance relatives and friends should be invited to your wedding no matter how far away they live.

Write or call them as soon as you have selected your date. In this way, they can plan their vacation time and travel arrangements as early as possible.

Long-distance invitations should be sent out eight weeks prior to the wedding instead of the usual six weeks.

If they require hotel accommodations, select hotels near your *reception* site. Be sure to inquire about special packages and group rates at the hotel.

As you receive the invitation replies, send information on the hotel accommodations. Major hotels provide brochures with all of the necessary details.

If available, arrange sleeping accommodations at local relatives' and friends' homes. Use this space below to record all locations and arrangements.

RELATIVES'/FRIENDS' HOMES AVAILABLE			
Guest	Address of Home	Phone	Date Needed

OUT-OF-TOWN GUEST ARRANGEMENTS

GUESTS _____

Arrival date/time _____

Staying at _____ Cost _____

Room # _____ Phone _____

Departure date/time _____

Scheduled driver _____

GUESTS _____

Arrival date/time _____

Staying at _____ Cost _____

Room # _____ Phone _____

Departure date/time _____

Scheduled driver _____

GUESTS _____

Arrival date/time _____

Staying at _____ Cost _____

Room # _____ Phone _____

Departure date/time _____

Scheduled driver _____

GUESTS _____

Arrival date/time _____

Staying at _____ Cost _____

Room # _____ Phone _____

Departure date/time _____

Scheduled driver _____

GUESTS _____

Arrival date/time _____

Staying at _____ Cost _____

Room # _____ Phone _____

Departure date/time _____

Scheduled driver _____

Attendants' Gifts

Things to know about giving gifts to your bridal party attendants.

☐ It is customary to give your attendants a small gift. This token of appreciation is usually an item that is a momento of the occasion.

☐ Be sure to also remember any car drivers or other special people who helped you with an important task in your wedding planning. The gifts can be given at the bridal luncheon, bachelor party, or the rehearsal dinner party.

☐ The gifts to the attendants can be identical, or the same amount of money can be used to buy individual gifts with special meaning.

☐ It is also a nice gesture to engrave the gift with the wedding date and the recipient's initials.

☐ Do include a card with a sincere note of gratitude.

☐ Consider a party to acquaint the bridesmaids and groomsmen before the wedding day.

☐ Also consider a thank-you party after the honeymoon. Invite all of the attendants over to your home to see your wedding gifts and the first showing of your wedding video.

RECORD OF GIFT IDEAS

| **BRIDESMAIDS** |
| (and other women to thank) |

For _____

Gift _____ Cost _____

Purchased at _____

For _____

Gift _____ Cost _____

Purchased at _____

For _____

Gift _____ Cost _____

Purchased at _____

For _____

Gift _____ Cost _____

Purchased at _____

For _____

Gift _____ Cost _____

Purchased at _____

For _____

Gift _____ Cost _____

Purchased at _____

For _____

Gift _____ Cost _____

Purchased at _____

For _____

Gift _____ Cost _____

Purchased at _____

For _____

Gift _____ Cost _____

Purchased at _____

ttendants' Gift Ideas

a framed photo of the wedding party
wallet
key case
pen and pencil set
theater/concert tickets
stationery
cup or mug
travel alarm clock
jewelry
sports event tickets

tie bars
tie tacks
handbags/gloves
a compact case
wine
appointment book
a gold charm/bracelet
perfume
gift certificates

RECORD OF GIFT IDEAS

GROOMSMEN (and other men to thank)

For _____

Gift _____ Cost _____

Purchased at _____

For _____

Gift _____ Cost _____

Purchased at _____

For _____

Gift _____ Cost _____

Purchased at _____

For _____

Gift _____ Cost _____

Purchased at _____

For _____

Gift _____ Cost _____

Purchased at _____

For _____

Gift _____ Cost _____

Purchased at _____

For _____

Gift _____ Cost _____

Purchased at _____

For _____

Gift _____ Cost _____

Purchased at _____

For _____

Gift _____ Cost _____

Purchased at _____

$\mathcal{P}$re-Wedding Parties

THE BRIDAL LUNCHEON

This "Ladies Only" party is attended by the bride, bridesmaids, mothers, and grandmothers.

It can be a brunch, a formal dinner, a pajama party, or an afternoon tea. It is traditionally held during the week prior to the wedding day.

A special bride's cake may be served as the dessert. Traditionally, a thimble or wedding ring is baked into the cake. The person who gets the trinket in her piece of cake is said to be the next to marry.

The bride may also give the attendants their gifts at this party.

GUEST LIST FOR THE BRIDAL LUNCHEON

Name	Address	Phone	Response

ESTIMATES FOR THE BRIDAL LUNCHEON

ESTIMATE #1	ESTIMATE #2
Party Site_____	Party Site_____
Address_____	Address_____
Telephone_____	Telephone_____
Number of Guests_____	Number of Guests_____
Date of Party_____	Date of Party_____
Time_____	Time_____
MENU CHOICES COST	MENU CHOICES COST
#1_____	#1_____
_____	_____
_____	_____
_____	_____
#2_____	#2_____
_____	_____
_____	_____
_____	_____
#3_____	#3_____
_____	_____
_____	_____
_____	_____
Drinks (average cost)_____	Drinks (average cost)_____
Entertainment	Entertainment
_____	_____
_____	_____
Decorations_____	Decorations_____
Misc._____	Misc._____
Room charge_____	Room charge_____
Gratuity_____	Gratuity_____
Estimated Total_____	Estimated Total_____
Deposit required_____	Deposit required_____

THE BACHELOR PARTY

This party, which traditionally celebrates the end of the groom's bachelorhood, is held a few days before the wedding so that the groom and other members of the bridal party can recover.

This party is usually hosted by the best man. It can be a formal dinner, a casual lunch, a night on the town, or an informal get-together.

Although women *never* attend this party, it is correct for the bride to help with its planning as well as the food preparation and serving.

The groom may also give the attendants their gifts at this party.

GUEST LIST FOR THE BACHELOR PARTY

Name	Address	Phone	Response

ESTIMATES FOR THE BACHELOR PARTY

ESTIMATE #1	ESTIMATE #2
Party Site_____	Party Site_____
Address_____	Address_____
Telephone_____	Telephone_____
Number of Guests_____	Number of Guests_____
Date of Party_____	Date of Party_____
Time_____	Time_____
MENU CHOICES COST	MENU CHOICES COST
#1_____	#1_____
#2_____	#2_____
#3_____	#3_____
Drinks (average cost)_____	Drinks (average cost)_____
Entertainment	Entertainment
Decorations_____	Decorations_____
Misc._____	Misc._____
Room charge_____	Room charge_____
Gratuity_____	Gratuity_____
Estimated Total_____	Estimated Total_____
Deposit required_____	Deposit required_____

109

THE REHEARSAL DINNER PARTY

- This celebration takes place after the rehearsal on the day before the wedding day.
- This party is usually hosted by the groom's parents. However, close friends, relatives, or godparents may host this event.
- Everyone who is participating in the wedding ceremony is invited to attend this party.
- The rehearsal party can be *any* kind of party—not just a dinner.
- Invitations can be informal handwritten notes or a telephone invitation.
- The attendants' gifts may be given at this party.
- Special toasts can also be included.

GUEST LIST FOR THE REHEARSAL DINNER PARTY

Name	Address	Phone	Response

ESTIMATES FOR THE REHEARSAL DINNER PARTY

ESTIMATE #1	ESTIMATE #2
Party Site_____	Party Site_____
Address_____	Address_____
Telephone_____	Telephone_____
Number of Guests_____	Number of Guests_____
Date of Party_____	Date of Party_____
Time_____	Time_____
MENU CHOICES COST	MENU CHOICES COST
#1_____	#1_____
_____	_____
_____	_____
_____	_____
#2_____	#2_____
_____	_____
_____	_____
_____	_____
#3_____	#3_____
_____	_____
_____	_____
_____	_____
Drinks (average cost)_____	Drinks (average cost)_____
Entertainment	Entertainment
_____	_____
_____	_____
Decorations_____	Decorations_____
Misc._____	Misc._____
Room charge_____	Room charge_____
Gratuity_____	Gratuity_____
Estimated Total_____	Estimated Total_____
Deposit required_____	Deposit required_____

REHEARSAL DINNER PARTY PROGRAM

Party will be held at _____

Date _____ Time _____

BEFORE DINNER TOASTS   **Given By:**

_____

_____

_____

_____

DINNER MENU SERVED

_____

_____

_____

_____

AFTER DINNER TOASTS   **Given By:**

_____

_____

_____

_____

SPECIAL PRESENTATIONS:

_____

_____

_____

_____

BRIDE AND GROOM APPRECIATION GIFTS:

_____

_____

_____

_____

Special Notes About This Month's Details

Month of: _____

SUNDAY	MONDAY	TUESDAY	WEDNESDAY	THURSDAY	FRIDAY	SATURDAY

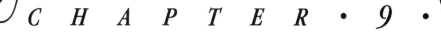

MONTHS BEFORE

Newspaper Wedding Announcements

•

Reception Etiquette

•

Traditional Customs

ewspaper Wedding Announcement

A guideline for publicly announcing your marriage

• Make a list of all the newspapers' names, addresses, and phone numbers that you wish to send this information to.

• Call publishers' offices to find out lead time needed and costs, if any.

• Make copies of the form to use as your information sheet. If you are including a photo, it should be an 8″ x 10″ black and white glossy print that has been professionally photographed.

• Be sure to include your name and full address on the back of the photo if you want it returned.

• Make sure to insert cardboard for support and label the envelope "PHOTO—DO NOT BEND."

Newspaper _____   Photograph Included ☐   Return to:

Address _____   Name _____

Editor's Name _____   Address _____

Release Date _____   City _____ State _____ Zip _____

	BRIDE	GROOM
Full Name		
Parents' Names		
Address		
Parents' Name (if divorced)		
Address		
Schools Attended		
Special Clubs		
Military Service		
Employment		
Wedding Date		
Ceremony Site		

Officiant's Name _____

Description of Bridal Gown _____

_____

_____

_____

Wedding Bouquet Description _____

_____

Honeymoon Destination _____

Residence after Wedding _____
                                     (city)   (state)

Reception Etiquette

SPECIAL TASKS CHECKLIST

Allow your attendants, ushers, family, and friends to help you by performing special tasks that you cannot do yourself.

SPECIAL TASK	PERFORMED BY
Help set up entertainment/equipment	
Distribute ceremony programs	
Help videographer	
Guest book signing	
Ring pillow arrangements	
Pay clergyman	
Pass out rice to toss	
Set up gift table	
Arrange place cards/special seating	
Carry bridal first-aid kit	
Move gifts after reception	
Bring unity candle	
Give fee to musicians	
Pay reception balance	
Move top layer of cake	
Store cake in freezer	
Collect extra favors/accessories	
Take wedding gown to cleaners	
Return groom's tuxedo	
Take bouquet to be preserved	
Develop film	
Drive wedding couple to airport	
Deposit money in bank	
Watch house while honeymooning	
Cut announcement out of paper	
Return any rental equipment	

Traditional Customs

The following are activities and customs that are a traditional part of a wedding reception. Perhaps you may wish to include them in your celebration.

THE RECEIVING LINE

The receiving line is a lineup of people from the wedding party who welcome the guests as they enter the reception site. This custom allows distant relatives and friends to be personally introduced.

The typical receiving line order is:

| Mother of Bride | Father of Groom | Mother of Groom | Father of Bride | Groom | Bride | Maid of Honor | Brides Maid | Brides Maid |

THE FIRST DANCE

Either after the bridal couple has arrived or after the meal is finished, the band plays the wedding couple's favorite song. The band leader introduces the new "Mr. and Mrs._____" to the guests. The couple comes forward and dances alone in the center of the dancefloor.

As the song continues, the parents and other members of the wedding party are introduced and join in the dancing.

SPECIAL SEATING

A special "Head Table," as pictured here, can be set up for the bridal party. This table can also be elevated on a low platform stage, so that all of the guests can easily view the bridal party during the meal.

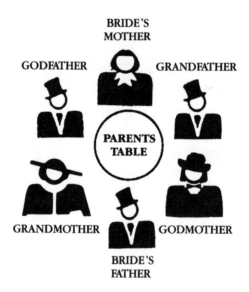

Individual place cards can be set at tables reserved for special guests.

Parents may be placed at "Parents Tables" to share dinner with their relatives and close friends.

Prearranged seating requires thall all tables are numbered. A seating chart is usually posted to direct guests to their individual seats. All seats are usually marked with place cards.

THE WEDDING TOAST

When all guests have been seated, a champagne or sparkling wine is served to all. It is traditional that the best man propose the first toast to the wedding couple.

The groom replies with thanks and toasts the parents.

Other toasts may be made by any family member or friend.

All telegrams or other messages may also be read aloud at this time.

TOASTS FROM AROUND THE WORLD		
Nation	**Toast**	**Pronunciation**
American	Happy Days To Your Good Health	
Austrian	Prosit	Proh' zit
Polish	Na Zdravie	Nah Zdroh' vee yeh
English	Cheers	
French	A Votre Sante	A Votre Shan' tay
Greek	Eis Igian	Ees igee' an
Irish	Salinte	Slahn' she
Hebrew	L'chayim	Leh hah' yim
Italian	A la Salute	Ah lah Sa loo' tay
Japanese	Kampai	Kahm pah' ee
Spanish	Salud	Sa lood'

CUTTING THE CAKE

This age-old custom symbolizes the willingness of the wedding couple to share their worldly goods together. The cutting of cake together and feeding each other a piece of it is said to ensure future happiness.

Today, the wedding cake is usually served as the dessert of the wedding meal.

The top layer of the cake is frozen and saved for the couple's first wedding anniversary celebration.

THROWING THE BOUQUET

All single women gather to the center of the dancefloor and form a circle around the bride. The bride may or may not be blindfolded; she throws her bouquet over her shoulder. The woman who catches this bouquet is said to be the next to marry.

TOSSING THE GARTER

This custom allows the groom to be encircled by all of the single men. He tosses the bride's garter over his shoulder. Following this, the man who caught the garter dances with the woman who caught the bouquet as the reception guests applaud.

THE LAST DANCE (THE CIRCLE OF LOVE)

The "Last Dance" of the evening calls for the wedding couple to again dance alone in the center of the dancefloor to their favorite song. At this time, reception guests form a circle of love around them and applaud them when the dance ends.

This is followed by a shower of rice (birdseed) as the wedding couple exits to their car.

Special Notes About This Month's Details

Month of: _____

SUNDAY	MONDAY	TUESDAY	WEDNESDAY	THURSDAY	FRIDAY	SATURDAY
___	___	___	___	___	___	___
___	___	___	___	___	___	___
___	___	___	___	___	___	___
___	___	___	___	___	___	___
___	___	___	___	___	___	___

CHAPTER · 10 ·

1

MONTH BEFORE

The Marriage License

·

The Wedding Rehearsal

The Marriage License

CHECKLIST FOR LICENSE INFORMATION

The marriage license legally binds the honorable intent of two people to become husband and wife. Regulations for the license vary from state to state.

To process a license you must:

☐ Apply for your license at least thirty days before the wedding.

☐ Call the marriage bureau (City Clerk's Office) in your city and make notes (below) of the specific requirements of your state.

☐ Both bride and groom must be present to apply.

☐ Be sure you have all of the required identification papers with you.

☐ After application is filled out and submitted, it is processed on the same day. Some states, however, require up to five days to process a license.

☐ The groom usually pays for the license. (Fee ranges from $10 to $30.)

☐ The license will be valid for between twenty and 180 days. Be sure you allow plenty of time.

☐ Remember—getting the license doesn't mean you are married. It must be signed by a civil or religious official, licensed by your state, to be legally valid.

LICENSE CHECKLIST

Date we should get our license _____

City Clerk's Office:

Address _____

Phone _____ Hours _____

We both need:

Identification (Driver's License) _____

Proof of Age (Birth Certificate) _____

Parental Consent _____

Citizenship Papers _____

Doctor's Certificate _____

Proof of Divorce or Annulment _____

Fee $ _____ Waiting Period _____ License valid for _____ days.

The Laws of Marriage

State	Age with parental consent		Age without consent		Physical exam & blood test for male and female				
	Male	Female	Male	Female	Maximum period between exam and license	Scope of medical exam	Waiting period Before license	After license
Alabama* 14a	14a	18	18	none	b	none	s
Alaska 16z	16z	18	18	none	b	3 da., w	none
Arizona 16z	16z	18	18	none	none	none	none
Arkansas 17c	16c	18	18	none	none	v	none
California . . . . aa	aa	18	18	30 da., w	bb	none	h
Colorado* 16z	16z	18	18	none	none	none	s
Connecticut 16z	16z	18	18	none	bb	4 da., w	ttt
Delaware 18c	16c	18	18	none	none	none	e, s
Florida . . . . 16a, c	16a, c	18	18	none	b	3 da.	s
Georgia* . . . . aa	aa	16	16	none	b	3 da., g	s*
Hawaii 16d	16d	18	18	none	b	none	none
Idaho* 16z	16z	18	18	none	bb	none	none
Illinois 16	16	18	18	30 da.	b, n	none	ee
Indiana 17c	17c	18	18	none	bb	72 hrs.	t
Iowa* 18z	18z	18	18	none	none	3 da., v	tt
Kansas* 18z	18z	18	18	none	none	3 da., w	none
Kentucky . . . . 18c, z	18c, z	18	18	none	none	none	none
Louisiana 18z	18z	18	18	10 da.	b	72 hrs., w	none
Maine 16z	16z	18	18	none	none	3 da., v, w	h
Maryland . . . . 16c, f	16c, f	18	18	none	none	48 hrs., w	ff
Massachusetts 16d	16	18	18	60 da.	bb	3 da., v	none
Michigan . . . . 16c, d	16c	18	18	30 da.	b	3 da., w	none
Minnesota 16z	16z	18	18	none	none	5 da., w	none
Mississippi . . . . aa	aa	17gg	15gg	30 da.	b	3 da., w	none
Missouri 15d, 18z	15d, 18z	18	18	none	none	none	none
Montana* 16	16	18	18	none	b	none	ff
Nebraska 17	17	18	18	none	bb	none	none
Nevada 16z	16z	18	18	none	none	none	none
New Hampshire . . . 14j	13j	18	18	30 da.	b, l	3 da., v	h
New Jersey . . . . 16z, c	16z, c	18	18	30 da.	b	72 hrs., w	s
New Mexico 16d	16d	18	18	30 da.	b	none	none
New York 14j	14j	18	18	none	nn	none	24 hrs., w, l
North Carolina . . . . 16c, g	16c, g	18	18	none	m	v	none
North Dakota 16	16	18	18	none	none	none	t
Ohio* . . . . 18c, z	16c, z	18	18	30 da.	b	5 da.	t, w
Oklahoma* 16c	16c	18	18	30 da., w	b	none	s
Oregon 17	17	18	18	none	none	3 da., w	none

continued . . .

State	Age with parental consent		Age without consent		Physical exam & blood test for male and female			
	Male	Female	Male	Female	Maximum period between exam and license	Scope of medical exam	Waiting period Before license	After license
Pennsylvania*	16d	16d	18	18	30 da.	b	3 da., w	t
Puerto Rico	18c, d, z	16c, d, z	21	21	none	b	none	none
Rhode Island*	18d	16d	18	18	none	bb	none	none
South Carolina*	16c	14c	18	18	none	none	1 da.	none
South Dakota	16c	16c	18	18	none	none	none	tt
Tennesee	16d	16d	18	18	none	none	3 da., cc	s
Texas*	14j, k	14j, k	18	18	none	none	none	s
Utah	14	14	18x	18x	30 da.	b	none	s
Vermont	16z	16z	18	18	30 da.	b	3 da., w	none
Virginia	16a, c	16a, c	18	18	none	b	none	t
Washington	17d	17d	18	18	none	bbb	3 da.	t
West Virginia	18c	18c	18	18	none	b	3 da., w	none
Wisconsin	16	16	18	18	none	b	5 da., w	s
Wyoming	16d	16d	18	18	none	bb	none	none
Dist. of Columbia*	16a	16a	18	18	30 da., w	b	3 da., w	none

*Indicates 1987 common-law marriage recognized; in many states, such marriages are only recognized if entered into many years before. (a) Parental consent not required if minor was previously married. (aa) No age limits. (b) Venereal diseases. (bb) Venereal diseases and Rubella (for female). In Colorado, Rubella for female under 45 and Rh type. (bbb) No medical exam required; however, applicants must have affidavit showing non-affliction of contagious venereal disease. (c) Younger parties may obtain license in case of pregnancy or birth of child. (cc) Unless parties are over 18 years of age. (d) Younger parties must obtain license in special circumstances. (e) Residents before expiration of 24-hour waiting period; non-residents formerly residents, before expiration of 96-hour waiting period; others 96 hours. (ee) License effective 1 day after issuance, unless court orders otherwise, valid for 60 days only. (f) If parties are under 16 years of age, proof of age and the consent of parents in person is required. If a parent is ill, an affidavit by the incapacitated parent and a physician's affidavit to that effect required. (ff) License valid for 180 days only. (g) Unless parties are 18 years of age or more, or female is pregnant, or applicants are the parents of a living child born out of wedlock. (gg) Notice to parents necessary if parties are under 21. (h) License valid for 90 days only. (j) Parental consent and/or permission of judge required. (k) Below age of consent parties need parental consent and permission of judge. (i) With each certificate issued to couples, a list of family planning agencies and services available to them is provided. (m) Mental incompetence, infectious tuberculosis, venereal diseases and Rubella (certain counties only). (n) Venereal diseases; test for sickle cell anemia given at request of examining physician. (nn) Tests for sickle cell anemia may be required for certain applicants. Marriage prohibited unless it is established that procreation is not possible. (p) If one or both parties are below the age for marriage without parental consent (3 day waiting period). (s) License valid for 30 days only. (t) License valid for 60 days only. (tt) License valid for 20 days only. (ttt) License is valid for 65 days. (v) Parties must file notice of intention to marry with local clerk. (w) Waiting period may be avoided. (x) Authorizes counties to provide for premarital counseling as a requisite to issuance of license to persons under 19 and persons previously divorced. (y) Marriages by proxy are valid. (yy) Proxy marriages are valid under certain conditions. (z) Younger parties may marry with parental consent and/or permission of judge. In Connecticut, judicial approval. (zz) With consent of court.

From *The World Almanac & Book of Facts,* 1991 edition, copyright © Pharos Books 1990, New York, NY 10166.

he Wedding Rehearsal

THE REHEARSAL CHECKLIST

☐ All members of the wedding party *must* attend the rehearsal.

☐ Copies of the ceremony program should be provided to all participants for the rehearsal.

☐ Follow the instructions of the officiant for the specific details regarding your ceremony.

☐ Rehearse with music if possible.

☐ Do not overrehearse the children in the wedding party.

☐ Tell all ushers to arrive at least one hour early on the wedding day.

Traditional Jewish ——————————

PROCESSIONAL TO THE ALTAR
(Before the Ceremony)

RECESSIONAL FROM THE ALTAR
(After the Ceremony)

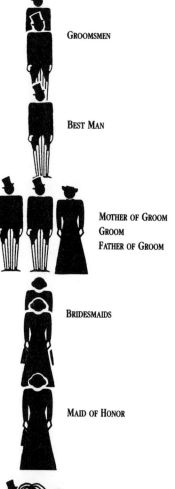

GROOMSMEN

BEST MAN

MOTHER OF GROOM
GROOM
FATHER OF GROOM

BRIDESMAIDS

MAID OF HONOR

MOTHER OF BRIDE
BRIDE
FATHER OF BRIDE

BRIDESMAIDS
GROOMSMEN

MAID OF HONOR
BEST MAN

MOTHER & FATHER
OF GROOM

MOTHER & FATHER
OF BRIDE

BRIDE & GROOM

Traditional Christian

PROCESSIONAL TO THE ALTAR
(Before the Ceremony)

RECESSIONAL FROM THE ALTAR
(After the Ceremony)

MOTHER & FATHER
OF GROOM

GROOM

BEST MAN

MOTHER & FATHER
OF BRIDE

GROOMSMEN

BRIDESMAIDS
GROOMSMEN

BRIDESMAIDS

MAID OF HONOR
BEST MAN

MAID OF HONOR

FLOWER GIRL
RING BEARER

FLOWER GIRL
RING BEARER

BRIDE

FATHER OF BRIDE

BRIDE & GROOM

AT THE CEREMONY

The first six pews on each side of the center aisle are usually reserved for special family members. These pews can be marked with ribbons. List below the names of those who will be seated in the reserved section. If any parents are divorced, follow the RIGHT SIDE for proper seating. Make a copy to give to the head usher at the rehearsal.

BRIDE'S SIDE (THE LEFT SIDE)

Mother & Father   1

Names_____

_____

Sisters & Brothers   2

Names_____

_____

Grandparents   3

Names_____

_____

Godparents   4

Names_____

_____

Special Guests   5

Names_____

_____

Special Guests   6

Names_____

_____

GROOM'S SIDE (THE RIGHT SIDE)

1 Mother & Husband/Companion

   Names_____

   _____

2 Sisters & Brothers

   Names_____

   _____

3 Father & Wife/Companion

   Names_____

   _____

4 Grandparents

   Names_____

   _____

5 Godparents

   Names_____

   _____

6 Special Guests

   Names_____

   _____

• During the ceremony, the bride's family and friends sit on the LEFT side of the center aisle. • The groom and groomsmen wear their boutonnieres on their LEFT side. • The bride and groom place their wedding rings on their LEFT hands. • The bride walks down the aisle on her escort's LEFT side.

• During the ceremony, the groom's family and friends sit on the RIGHT side of the center aisle. • The ushers offer each female guest their RIGHT arm as they escort her to her seat. • The bride wears her engagement ring on her RIGHT hand throughout the wedding ceremony.

Special Notes About This Month's Details

Month of: _____

SUNDAY	MONDAY	TUESDAY	WEDNESDAY	THURSDAY	FRIDAY	SATURDAY
_____	_____	_____	_____	_____	_____	_____
_____	_____	_____	_____	_____	_____	_____
_____	_____	_____	_____	_____	_____	_____
_____	_____	_____	_____	_____	_____	_____
_____	_____	_____	_____	_____	_____	_____

C H A P T E R · 11 ·

THE "QUICKIE" MARRIAGE

*Planning a Wedding
in Twelve Weeks or Less!*

·

Ten Money-Saving Shortcuts

The "Quickie" Wedding

A wedding is a special occasion. Knowing "how-to" when every minute counts will allow you to plan this important event with no traditions being sacrificed.

The "Quickie" Wedding requires *teamwork*—with you, the bride, as the manager.

REMEMBER:

1. YOU ARE IN CHARGE!
This is your wedding, and it should be planned as *you* want it to be.

2. COMMUNICATION COUNTS.
Organize your helpers, and delegate tasks. Make a list of "things to do today" and update it daily.

3. DEADLINES ARE FOR KEEPING.
Meet your deadlines—it's the *only* way to get things done.

4. PRAISE AND THANK YOU are *all important* words.

5. KNOW WHEN YOU MUST DO IT YOURSELF!
Pace yourself—plan to do one major task each day.

When circumstances dictate that your wedding must be planned in twelve weeks instead of twelve months, follow this priority checklist, and your planning will be hassle-free.

Most Important Advice: *Keep it SMALL, SIMPLE, AND DIGNIFIED.*

TWELVE WEEKS BEFORE THE WEDDING:

- [ ] 1. Set the date and time.
- [ ] 2. Meet with parents and organize budget.
- [ ] 3. Hold engagement party and announce plans.
- [ ] 4. Choose the type of wedding formality you want.
- [ ] 5. Visit the clergy member or judge. Make ceremony and rehearsal arrangements.
- [ ] 6. Reserve the reception site.
- [ ] 7. Meet and hire the caterer.
- [ ] 8. Select your attendants.
- [ ] 9. Compile your guest lists.
- [ ] 10. Hire the photographer.
- [ ] 11. Choose your wedding dress and accessories.
- [ ] 12. Register at the bridal registry.

TEN WEEKS BEFORE THE WEDDING:

- [ ] 1. Order the invitations.
- [ ] 2. Select the florist.
- [ ] 3. Hire the musicians for the ceremony and reception.
- [ ] 4. Shop for bridesmaids dresses and accessories.
- [ ] 5. Select the men's formal wear.
- [ ] 6. Make honeymoon arrangements.
- [ ] 7. Reserve the restaurant for the rehearsal dinner.

EIGHT WEEKS BEFORE THE WEDDING:

☐ 1. Address the invitations.

☐ 2. Select the attendants' gifts.

☐ 3. Select a videographer (optional).

☐ 4. Reserve a limousine.

☐ 5. Contact newspapers about announcement.

SIX WEEKS BEFORE THE WEDDING:

☐ 1. Mail invitations.

☐ 2. Reserve all rental equipment.

☐ 3. Make hotel reservations for out-of-town guests.

FOUR WEEKS BEFORE THE WEDDING:

☐ 1. Apply for your marriage license.

☐ 2. Buy wedding gifts for each other.

☐ 3. Plan bridal luncheon.

☐ 4. Have final fitting.

☐ 5. Have formal portrait taken.

☐ 6. Plan rehearsal party—notify all.

TWO WEEKS BEFORE THE WEDDING:

☐ 1. Send information to newspapers.

☐ 2. Schedule your hair and nail appointment.

☐ 3. Prepare toasts for rehearsal dinner and reception.

☐ 4. Confirm honeymoon arrangements.

ONE WEEK BEFORE THE WEDDING:

☐ 1. Make a list of last-minute details.

☐ 2. Pack for your honeymoon.

☐ 3. Give caterer final guest count.

☐ 4. Prepare announcements for mailing immediately after wedding day.

☐ 5. Arrange for pick-up of wedding gown and formal wear.

☐ 6. Confirm all deliveries and arrangements.

☐ 7. Attend rehearsal and rehearsal dinner.

WEDDING DAY:

☐ 1. Arrive *on time*—an organized and beautiful bride!

Ten Money-Saving Shortcuts

INVITATIONS

Design your own invitations, and have them typeset and printed at a local instant printer. Most have a large selection of colored paper and envelopes.

PHOTOGRAPHY

Purchase a photo album at a local stationery or department store. Arrange your wedding picture story in it.

MUSIC

Use taped cassettes, and hire someone to organize and play them throughout the reception.

HONEYMOON

Plan just a "weekend getaway" for now and a long honeymoon when time permits. Many resorts offer romantic weekend packages. Ask any travel agent for this information.

RECEPTION

Consider a reception at the ceremony site. Plan a brunch reception to save tremendously on food costs. Use paper tablecloths and napkins in the bridal colors.

BRIDAL ATTIRE

Rent or borrow a friend's wedding gown. Consider a resale shop, or wear a family "heirloom" gown. Sewing a gown is a real money saver.

ATTENDANTS' ATTIRE

Bridesmaids can wear daytime dresses purchased from the rack in a department store. Groomsmen can wear dark suits with ties that are the same color as the maids dresses.

FLOWERS

Use potted flowers for the altar instead of floral arrangements. Share the cost of these flowers with another bride who will marry on the same day.

CAKE

Stack two bakery purchased iced layer cakes of varying sizes, and decorate with fresh flowers and a cake topper.

DECORATIONS

Festive pew markers can be made using bows made of wide white ribbon.

Special Notes About This Month's Details

Month of: _____

SUNDAY	MONDAY	TUESDAY	WEDNESDAY	THURSDAY	FRIDAY	SATURDAY
_____	_____	_____	_____	_____	_____	_____
_____	_____	_____	_____	_____	_____	_____
_____	_____	_____	_____	_____	_____	_____
_____	_____	_____	_____	_____	_____	_____
_____	_____	_____	_____	_____	_____	_____

AFTER THE "BIG DAY"

Thank-You Notes

•

Wedding Announcements

•

Changing Your Name

•

Preserving Your Gown

Thank-You Notes

Use this guideline to help you to write a warm and personal message of appreciation.

* A note should be written for each shower and wedding gift that you receive.

* Black or blue ink are the most readable colors to use.

* Each thank-you note should be *handwritten*. They may be brief, but they should be interesting.

* *Always* name the gift received in your note.
  Example: "The travel iron you sent, etc."

* *Never* use preprinted thank-you cards.

* Gifts of money can be acknowledged by saying how you will use the money.
  Example: "How thoughtful of you to remember us with a gift of money. We plan to use it to purchase a microwave oven that every working couple needs. Thanks again for your generosity. Love."

* Address the person as you always do.
  Example: "Dear Jim," "Dear Mr. and Mrs. Johnson." In the case of your fiancé's (husband's) relatives, address them as he knows them.

* Thank-you notes are signed by *one person*—the writer. But it is proper to mention your husband.
  Example: "John and I were thrilled with the crystal wine glasses."

* Close your note with the same form with which you began.
  Example: "Dear Ken," "Dear Mary." Close with—Love, Fondly. "Dear Mr. & Mrs. Smith." Close with—Sincerely yours.

* BE PROMPT! All thank-you notes should be sent out within one month after the wedding day.

* A group gift from co-workers who will not attend the wedding should be thanked with *one* note of appreciation to all.

* A group gift from family or close friends should be thanked with a personal note to everyone who contributed.

• If you receive a gift you plan to return, thank the giver anyway and keep your intentions to yourself. (The same applies for duplicate gifts.)

• Sign each thank-you note with the new name you have chosen with your marriage. This is an easy way to let everyone know how you wish to be addressed for the future.

• Write as you would speak. Read your note out loud. Correct it so that it resembles how you would say it if you were speaking to that person.

• When writing your notes, keep thinking that you will be making someone just as happy with this note of appreciation as they made you with their gift.

Wedding Announcements

ANNOUNCEMENT LIST

Wedding announcements are sent to all family and friends that could not be invited to the wedding. They are mailed immediately after the wedding.

NAME / ADDRESS / CITY, STATE, ZIP	COMMENTS		
NAME			
ADDRESS			
CITY, STATE, ZIP			

NAME	COMMENTS		
ADDRESS			
CITY, STATE, ZIP			

hanging Your Name

Guidelines to follow when changing your name

• Today, many brides combine names by using their maiden name as their middle name and adopting their husband's surname.

• Whatever name you decide on, it is absolutely necessary that you *consistently* sign that name on all important identification and all legal documents.

• Some agencies may require that a copy of the marriage license be sent with a written notification.

• Some agencies may require a visit to the local office in your city with a copy of the marriage license.

• Some agencies can be notified by simply including a name change on the monthly statement or bill.

A R E A S   O F   N O T I F I C A T I O N

Driver's License	School and/or Employer's Records
Car Registration	Post Offices
Social Security	Investments
Voter Registration	Property Titles
Passport	Leases
Bank Accounts	Wills
Credit Cards	Beneficiaries
Insurance Policies	

Most state agencies require that a written notice of a name change be sent to them. Use this standard letter for anyone you may need to notify.

Date _____

Dear _____ ,

    We would like to inform you of our upcoming marriage and the changes that will be necessary in our names and addresses.

My account number is _____ .

_____   _____
Groom's Full Name   Bride's Full Name

_____   _____
Groom's Current Address   Bride's Current Address

_____   _____
City   State   Zip   City   State   Zip

CHANGED TO:

_____
Husband's Full Name

_____
Wife's Full Name

_____
New Address

_____
City   State   Zip

AFTER

_____ , 19 _____

PLEASE NOTE: _____ We plan to continue service.

                       _____ We will discontinue service after _____ .

                       _____ Send all forms needed to include my spouse on my policy/account.

I can be reached at (   ) _____ if you have any questions.

                              Sincerely,

                             _____
                             Groom's Signature

                             _____
                             Bride's Signature

$\mathcal{P}$reserving Your Gown

Important tips to remember

* The wedding gown should be stored in a dark, dry place. Darkness is necessary, because light causes yellowing. Dryness is important, because moisture causes mildew.

* Have your gown professionally cleaned as soon as possible after the wedding. Common stains can become permanent in as short a period of time as a few days.

* Your stored gown can become your daughter's "heirloom" dress.

* Be sure to tell the cleaner about any stains on the garment. Food and beverages will *not* come out unless they are pretreated before the gown is cleaned.

* Discuss the beads, sequins, and laces with the cleaner. Glued-on beads and lace can fall off. Cleaners who specialize in wedding gowns use a gentler solvent to protect the fabric from damage.

* Be sure to examine the gown after it is cleaned.

* A cellophane window in a box is *not recommended*. It allows light to come in and yellow the garment. Request a solid cardboard box.

* The cost of professionally cleaning a wedding gown ranges from $75 to $150.

$\mathcal{W}$edding Memories to Cherish

The day we met _____ .

Our first date was _____ .

We became engaged on _____ 19 _____ .

He asked me to marry him by

_____

_____ .

Our wedding date _____ .

I awoke at _____ on my wedding day.

The wedding day weather was _____ .

My wedding hairstyle was done by _____ .

I was escorted down the aisle by _____ .

Special traditions we celebrated in our wedding were

_____

_____

_____ .

My something old was _____ , something new _____ ,

something borrowed _____ , something blue _____ .

I threw my bouquet to _____ .

The garter was caught by _____ .

Our wedding song was _____ .

Our last dance was at _____ o'clock.

Our wedding night was spent at _____ .

We honeymooned in _____ .

The funniest thing that happened during our honeymoon

_____

_____ .

The most romatic part of our honeymoon was

_____

_____ .

Ready References

Ceremony Site_____ Address_____

Officiant_____ Phone_____

Reception Site_____ Address_____

Caterer_____ Phone_____

Invitations_____

Contact_____ Phone_____

Calligrapher_____ Phone_____

Florist_____ Phone_____

Baker_____ Phone_____

Rental Equipment_____ Phone_____

Musicans (Ceremony)_____

Contact_____ Phone_____

Musicians (Reception)_____

Contact_____ Phone_____

Bridal Gown Store_____

Contact_____ Phone_____

Bridesmaids' Gowns_____

Contact_____ Phone_____

Formal Wear Rentals_____

Contact_____ Phone_____

Decorations_____

Contact_____ Phone_____

Limousine_____

Contact_____ Phone_____

Gift Registry_____

Contact_____ Phone_____

_____

Contact_____ Phone_____

_____

Contact_____ Phone_____